7/10

A Guide to Conducting Online Research

A Guide to Conducting Online Research

Ted J. Gaiser and Anthony E. Schreiner

Los Angeles • London • New Delhi • Singapore • Washington DC

SAGE Publications Ltd
1 Oliver's Yard
55 City Road
London EC1Y 1SP

SAGE Publications Inc.
2455 Teller Road
Thousand Oaks, California 91320

SAGE Publications India Pvt Ltd
B 1/I 1 Mohan Cooperative Industrial Area
Mathura Road
New Delhi 110 044

SAGE Publications Asia-Pacific Pte Ltd
33 Pekin Street #02-01
Far East Square
Singapore 048763

Library of Congress Control Number: 2008931849

British Library Cataloguing in Publication data

A catalogue record for this book is available from
the British Library

ISBN 978-1-4129-2289-0
ISBN 978-1-4129-2290-6 (pbk)

Typeset by C&M Digitals (P) Ltd, Chennai, India
Printed in Great Britain by The MPG Books Group
Printed on paper from sustainable resources

Mixed Sources
Product group from well-managed
forests and other controlled sources
www.fsc.org Cert no. SGS-COC-2953
FSC © 1996 Forest Stewardship Council

CONTENTS

ACKNOWLEDGEMENTS

It's extremely difficult to appropriately thank all of those who, at some point in the production of this book, generously contributed. A number of colleagues advised us, provided information, and gave constructive suggestions. Specifically, several of our colleagues at Boston College were extremely helpful. In particular, we would like to express our deep appreciation for the assistance of Rani Dalgin with the analytical sections of the book. Always the colleague, she was extremely helpful in providing both advice and support for our efforts. We would also like to thank Jared Del Rosso for references and suggestions, as he shared thoughts drawn from his own online research efforts. In addition, we'd like to express our gratitude to our colleagues Scott Kinder, Tom Babbin, Constantin Andronache, and Enid Karr.

We would like to express our gratitude to the editorial staff at Sage. We have received excellent editorial advice and guidance throughout the development of this book. In particularly, we'd like to express our deep appreciation to Patrick Brindle, Claire Lipscomb, and Imogen Roome.

We are grateful to our reviewers for their detailed suggestions and their formative advice in book organization and content. We appreciate the care they took in reading and responding to the proposal and manuscript.

And finally, we would not have been able to complete this book without support at home. We are grateful for advice and commentary on the book as well as encouragement for the project and tolerance of the time it took. We owe enormous debt to our life partners, Gesa Kirsch and Chuck Hornberger, for all of their support.

1 INTRODUCTION

In our roles as consultants, we often receive calls or email to discuss the development of an online research project. On one occasion, an individual, let's call her Jill, told me (TJG) that she was going to apply for a particular type of grant, and that she was interested in developing a web-based screening and intervention tool for the core component of the grant application. She expressed an interest in attending any courses I could recommend and was looking for some general advice regarding how to proceed with the development of her study.

First, how did she know to contact one of us? Why contact one of us? Jill contacted me through the usual word-of-mouth method. She had a friend, who knew a friend, who knew me. The friend of a friend knew that I had experience with online research, and so suggested that she get in touch with me for advice. In other words, Jill found me through professional networking. The networking, in itself, should say something to you. Information about developing online research isn't readily available, so researchers tend to track down colleagues who have some experience developing online studies, to seek their advice.

Jill contacted me for advice, and I suspect my responses were less than satisfying. In fact, they were probably a little discouraging. I noted that any courses I was aware of would typically cover technical tools such as PHP, which means they are designed and offered for computer programmers. I indicated that it might be useful to attend such courses, but that they might be difficult, and much of the material covered might not be directly applicable to her study. In addition, I indicated that there might be a course in the area of electronic research methods, but those courses were few and far between. Furthermore, while methodologically they will be interesting and useful, they are likely to lack the practical application of various technological tools to research methods. These latter courses are also unlikely to include hands-on assistance in the actual construction of an online study.

For some, my response would be a show-stopper. The lack of assistance available in developing online research often leads people back to more traditional forms of research. In the case of this particular inquiry, Jill was persistent, suggesting that she might seek out a consultant to help her with her project.

Jill's next question to me was whether or not I had any advice for her about hiring a consultant. She was aware that I had experience managing technology consulting teams. In fact, both of us have worked with a number of individuals who have hired technical consultants to help them with their research projects, most often being asked to get involved after a consultant left the project or something had gone seriously wrong.

My suggestion to Jill was to find someone with technical skill who also had some research experience or suitable educational background, so that he or she would understand what she was trying to accomplish with her research. The ideal candidate for her, I surmised, would be someone with technical skill, research experience and academic credentials. This typically would mean a graduate student or intern who has programming or other technical experience. I cautioned, however, that this type of person is usually difficult to find, may already be employed, and/or is likely to be transient. This last point of being transient, meaning only available for a limited period of time, I noted, should not be considered lightly. A project can run into considerable snags when the main technical architect is no longer available. Replacement staff may not understand what was initially developed, source files may not be well organized or, worse, files may be missing. Ultimately, everything ends up on hold until the project can be put back on track.

It is very common for researchers to find themselves in a quandary about how to proceed with an online research project. They may be clear that their research population is best reached online. They may have colleagues encouraging them and making it all look so easy. They may have pressure to use technical tools to keep down project costs, for example by limiting the need for data entry. So they now face the question of what to do next. Who can help? What resources are available to them? Like this friend of a friend, they want to develop an online study, but need assistance thinking through the various challenges related to their particular needs, before they start developing the study.

About this book

It is out of the preceding type of experience that this book was developed. Our focus and purpose is to provide you, the reader, with a research consultant. Using our consulting experience and knowledge of best practices, we have developed a guide to help answer your questions. This book isn't meant to be read cover to cover like a novel or a textbook. It is more like a manual, though not your typical manual. Hopefully, you'll find a section that meets your particular needs. In some cases, you will discover practical step-by-step advice that is useful when embarking on a research study. When coverage is limited, either due to space or the depth of the issue, we'll also offer advice and direct you to resources that we hope will address your questions.

In short, the focus of this book is to support the use of technologies for research purposes. Our goal is to offer a collection of resource material to get the researcher started. We hope you'll think of it as an inexpensive consultant. As a resource, this book is meant to be the place to which a researcher turns when beginning to think through the practical aspects of developing an online research project, and where to seek information regarding the use of a particular technology for an online study. We believe that we accomplish our mission by providing you with technical explanations, instructions, self-help tips, useful links to other resources, references and case examples.

This book is not a methods text. There are a number of substantive online research methods texts available (e.g. Best & Krueger, 2004; Blank, Fielding & Lee, 2008; Jones, 1999). In addition, there is also a diverse body of research literature on a number of technology-related topics. Some books, for example, cover using computers for qualitative analysis (Miles & Huberman, 1994; Richards & Richards, 1991; Walker, 1993; Weitzman & Miles, 1995). Several authors have focused on the possibilities and subtleties of participant observation and online field work (Clodius, 1994; Hine, 2000; Ito, 1996; Markham, 1998; Nardi, 1996). In recent years this body of literature has been complemented by several books on online methods and the research of online social phenomena (e.g. Howard & Jones, 2004; Mann & Stewart, 2000). Adding to the growing body of literature are works that assist researchers in understanding the nuances and subtle differences in researching online (Hewson, Laurent, Yule & Vogel, 2003; Hine, 2000; Seale, 2004).

In addition, this book is not a software manual. People often think in terms of the "how-to for dummies" books such as *Windows XP for Dummies* (Harvey, 2004), or a technical manual such as *Adobe Photoshop CS Classroom in a Book*, a training workbook produced by a software developer or a licensee (2002). While there are several examples of how to do particular tasks and illustrations to highlight particular actions, none of the illustrations is meant to provide comprehensive training on a given subject or application. In all cases, they serve to make specific points about a technology and to provide some basics for a new user, so that a user can make educated decisions as he or she embarks on a new online research study.

We are aware that some readers may suggest that many software applications are intuitive today and relatively easy to use. They may also note that online services such as SurveyMonkey, a web-based survey service provider, make developing an online survey a breeze. And on those points they would be correct. While we may not be able to convince everyone to stick it out, we'll offer one thought. Just because there are statistical software packages that make it easy to run the numbers doesn't mean we're now all statisticians. While software gets easier to use, it's still necessary to have certain skills to be able to make informed choices. We believe this book can help the reader make many of those decisions.

At the risk of offending, it has been our experience that many users don't know what they don't know ... that is, until they find themselves in a bind with their project. They say things like, "Why didn't anyone warn me?" or "If I'd only known when I started this project." If you're unsure of the utility of this book, we encourage you to flip through a few chapters before putting it down. The most it will cost you is a few minutes of your time. On the other hand, if you learn something new, you may discover that we can save you considerable time.

Introduction to the content

Computer technology has greatly enhanced the ability to communicate, or interact, with others globally. Computer technology has also exposed people to new public and private spaces which constitute cyberspace, where humans and computers coexist (Fahey, 1994). When people discuss these spaces, they might be talking about any number of computer-mediate spaces. Electronic mail, or email, is one of the most basic of these "spaces." Email "is a store and forward method of composing, sending, storing, and receiving messages over electronic communication systems" (http://en.wikipedia.org/wiki/Email). A listserv discussion list enables people to send messages to a server that then distributes the message to all of the members. Then there are newsgroups (Usenet) where people participate in a kind of online conference by reading messages posted in a particular location and then posting their own contributions to a discussion. More recently, this type of interaction is seen in blogging.

> A blog is often a mixture of what is happening in a person's life and what is happening on the Web, a kind of hybrid diary/guide site, although there are as many unique types of blogs as there are people. People maintained blogs long before the term was coined, but the trend gained momentum with the introduction of automated published systems, most notably Blogger at blogger.com. Thousands of people use services such as Blogger to simplify and accelerate the publishing process. *Blogs* are alternatively called *web logs* or *weblogs*. However, "blog" seems less likely to cause confusion, as "web log" can also mean a server's log files. (http://www.marketingterms.com/dictionary/blog/)

Another space often inhabited in cyberspace is a Multi-user dungeon (MUD). MUDs have attracted the interest of academic scholars from many fields, including communications, sociology and law. They also have synthetic economies in different environments or what they would call different worlds. As stated in Wikipedia, "MUDs often have a fantasy setting, while many others are set in a science-fiction-based universe or themed on popular books, movies, animations, history, etc. Still others, especially those which are often referred to as MOOs, are used in distance education or to allow for virtual conferences" (http://en.wikipedia.org/wiki/MUD). The environments have become increasingly sophisticated and now can include virtual reality using 3-D animations in places such as Second Life (http://secondlife.com).

Many today are familiar with Internet Relay Chat (IRC) or instant messaging (IM). Both allow for synchronous interaction between individuals. IRC functions as an online conference call whereby many people can participate in a discussion simultaneously. While IM functions in a similar way, typically IM is thought of as a one-on-one type of interacting, while IRC is most often thought of as a multi-user environment. Instant communication is nowdays also available in the comment area of blogs, and at social sites such as Myspace, Facebook and Twitter.

As these various computer protocols enable individuals to interact in new ways, they open new spaces and forms of interaction that warrant research. Likewise, they make it possible to conduct research in new ways. An interview or focus group can be conducted asynchronously through email or synchronously in a chat room using an instant messaging or internet chat relay application. Any place where text is available on the internet represents the possibility for any number of qualitative studies such as narrative analysis and content analysis. Any place where people interact online represents a potential place where interactants can be observed and discussions can be analyzed. The locations for posting a survey or accessing potential study participants are virtually unlimited. In addition, accessible data abounds online from organizations such as the US Center for Disease Control (http://www.cdc.gov/datastatistics/), the International Monetary Fund (http://www.imf.org/external/data.htm) and the World Bank (http://www.worldbank.org/).

Blurring the boundaries
of traditional research

Before getting into the meat of our topic, it is worth making a few additional introductory remarks. Online researching has opened new environments to researchers that move beyond traditional research and challenge some of our notions of what it means to research, how people engage online, and so forth. A body of literature relative to assessing the value and experience in online learning environments has expanded to include games and simulations (Gibson, Aldrich & Prensky, 2007; Prensky, 2006). These environments not only offer new ways for learning, but also new ways in which to conduct research, creating simulations and testing conclusions (e.g. Gibson et al. 2007; Seo & Barrett, 2007).

One area often overlooked when reviewing the literature, but available nonetheless, is a growing body of work on ethical and legal considerations related to online research. For example, there are an increasing number of books on confidentiality (applied to research participants in this context) (e.g. Smedinghoff, 1996b). In the United States, any kind of health or medical related research requires adherence to federal regulations such as the Health Insurance Portability and Accountability Act (HIPAA) (http://www.hhs.gov/ocr/hipaa/), as well as adherence to copyright laws (e.g. Imparl, 2006; http://memory.loc.gov/learn/start/cite/index.html). It is safe to assume that many countries will have some kind of privacy requirement in the coming years, if they do not already have one. For example, in the UK, certain privacy matters are regulated by the governing body of the General Medical Council and the Health and Social Care Act. So, before beginning a study that may bring into question the management of personal data, it is a good practice to become familiar with current privacy regulations and legislation. A suggested starting point is discipline-specific literature.

Considering the literature

What is lacking in the growing body of literature on online research is a general self-help book. There is limited written guidance on how to bring together the technologies and the research methods. Researchers may be able to gain an appreciation for the subtleties of the online environment and the ways in which research questions need to be challenged, rethought and reshaped when researching online phenomena. They can also gain an appreciation of the kinds of challenges their methods will receive both in the research process and in academic research discourse. But what is not readily available to the researcher is how to actually conduct the research and apply the technologies. What technology should be used for conducting an interview? In what ways will digesting features support or challenge the research effort? Is there anything that can be done to guarantee the anonymity and security of a research participant in a chat room being used to conduct a focus group? How should firewall issues be handled? How to organize, manage, analyze and present data in online research? These are all questions that remain unaddressed in the current body of literature.

In our highly rationalized society, what material is available is specialized. You can find books and manuals that go into detail on specific topics such as making graphs (*Charts & Graphs in Microsoft Office Excel*, 2007), or how to use Internet Relay Chat (IRC) (*The Ultimate Guide to Internet Relay Chat*, Charalabidis, 1999). The books, like our professions, are presented as the experts on their respective topics. But what if you don't even know what technology you should use? Is it necessary to pick up every book on every different type of technology to determine which technology is right for your research purposes? We don't think so. We believe that there are times when the generalist is helpful.

We suggest you think of this book as your generalist. It focuses on addressing technical rather than methodological questions. It will provide technological advisement for conducting online research. This book will supply a link between various technologies and research methods, enabling the reader to embark on a study and address questions and concerns of his/her own particular research approach. Some of these topics, will be covered several times, with a differing emphasis on administrative, technological and potential ethical challenges.

This book is probably best used as a reference book. As noted previously, it was not created to be read from cover to cover like a manual. It focuses first on what questions to ask and how to prepare to conduct online research in the study design process. The subsequent chapters are organized around particular types of technologies such as email, chat and databases. As we cover these topics, there will be some discussion of specific products. We try to be current, but software and the World Wide Web are very fast changing fields, and new versions and entirely new products appear all the time, seemingly within the time it takes to describe a particular product. The final chapter touches upon some additional thoughts unique to research in the online environment, with the suggestion that there are topics beyond the scope of this book that are worth further consideration.

Cyberspace, the internet, the world wide web and other definitions

We often hear a number of words bandied about regarding the online environment. The three most prevalent are internet, cyberspace and World Wide Web. While not knowing their specific meanings might have limited impact on your research, it's possible you'll be more convincing as an online researcher if you can articulate their differences.

Cyberspace was coined by the novelist William Gibson and used to reflect the storage, modification and exchange of data. As noted in Wikipedia, it is often used synonymously with the internet, but it is not. Cyberspace, more accurately, reflects "objects and identities that exist largely within the communication network itself" (http://en.wikipedia.org/wiki/Cyberspace, accessed on 21 August 2007). The **internet**, on the other hand, refers to a network of networks through which the data of cyberspace are transmitted.

The **World Wide Web**, often referred to as 'the web', is a system of interlinked hypertext documents, the web sites and hot link references that reside on the internet. Communication of many sorts (text, still and motion pictures, sound) can be put on a web site, which is on a web server. One of the main innovations of the web (and the reason for the name) was the use of embedded hyperlinks from one document to another. The network of links between documents becomes the web. Web documents are viewed with a web browser. As a form of communication, the web is more like a broadcast in that there is no guarantee that the web site will be viewed by an intended recipient, or not viewed by an unintended recipient.

It was originally true that communication by web site was one way – from the author to the reader – but this is becoming less accurate as new web technologies allow for two-way exchanges. Web technologies have evolved from essentially one-way (server to browser) connections, to increasingly more interactive exchanges. First came forms, where end-users could enter a small amount of text into a field on the web page, or set a button or checkbox, and have that information returned to the server for processing, or storage. In parallel, technologies were developed for the visual (WYSIWYG) editing of web pages; and then for the synchronization of local copies of web documents with the server copies. At this point these have been combined, so that the user can be on a certain web site, and edit the appearance of the web page or create new web pages. In this way the web server/client relationship has become very interactive, and has allowed for the development of technologies such as weblogs and wikis; and of social networking sites like Facebook, MySpace, Flickr, YouTube and others. The impact on the nature of research and the evolving roles of participant and researcher remains to be seen.

Currently, the protocols for web sites are fairly standardized: HTTP (Hypertext Transport Protocol) for the transmission of data; HTML (Hypertext Markup Language) and in some cases CSS (Cascading Style Sheets) for the appearance of documents in a browser. HTML is most often written to a document with a text editor or a visual web site creation tool, but in either case it is stored as a static document on the web site. In some cases, for web sites that are created in response to some event or feedback from a user, a program is used to generate dynamically the HTML that is presented to the web browser. The communication from a web form to the web server is based on the CGI (Common Gateway Interface) standard. Information entered into text fields, or checkboxes, is returned via the CGI to the program running on the web server, which can then use the information to create a new web page. These programs can be written in any programming language, but are very often written in scripting languages such as perl, python, PHP and ruby. These languages have strong built-in tools for parsing text (in the data processing sense of separating continuous text into individual words or symbols of interest) and recognizing patterns, which is one of the main tasks of a CGI program, and additionally have tools for interacting with database software, which will be seen to be useful.

Other computer-based communications methods, such as Usenet and Chat, are increasingly being presented on top of a web-based interface as well. The Usenet is one of the oldest internet communication technologies. The server component is called a "news" server; it stores posted messages, and downloads them to any subscribed user who checks for new messages. It is organized by news groups, which have internet domain-like names, such as rec.food.cooking, or soc.culture.thai, etc. The user interfaces to a Usenet server with a news reader, which is often built into mail programs, as is the case for Outlook, Thunderbird, and others. Users subscribe to individual Usenet groups, and the news reader checks for any new messages in the group and downloads the header and contents to the client. Users may post to the group by composing a message and sending it. The technology and experience are very similar to an email listserver. The difference is that Usenet groups have no restrictions on who may subscribe and download. The Usenet first became searchable in the 1990s with DejaNews. Google has since purchased DejaNews and reformulated it as Google Groups. Now, other internet portals like Yahoo! provide group interaction as well.

Locating the internet in technological change

The transformation of communicative technologies has had a significant impact on society throughout the ages. From the early uses of art as a method of communication to the first written language of the Sumerians in 3200 BC, humans have changed, and been changed, through their ability to communicate. The introduction of the alphabet by the Greeks around 700 BC moved communication of ideas from the spoken to the written word (Castells, 2000: 355). Likewise, the development of the Gutenberg printing press in 1440 facilitated the eventual implementation of universal education and the mass production of literature (Buchanan, 1992: 173). In a similar fashion, the personal computer, a present-day technology, and the internet, the publicly accessible network for computer interaction, have impacted our understanding of work and leisure activities. People can work from home instead of going to an office space, conduct personal banking from home, and gather information on a wealth of topics with relative ease. In addition, they have given rise to new forms of social interaction and changed the ways in which people interact.

Interacting on the internet raises questions about subtle nuances in the way people communicate, shifting mannerisms and both challenging and enabling individuals to choose new ways in which to present themselves to others. These types of subtle shifts are fertile ground for research. Online interacting raises complications for researchers, in that they are unable to physically see a research participant's reactions to questions, for example, or, to have a context in which to appreciate and understand sarcasm. It is much easier for individuals to lurk in an online environment, limiting a researcher's ability to know who is actually "present" in the research process. While these topics raise important questions about the online environment, and challenges for conducting research online, they will not be addressed in depth in this book. Instead, we will direct you to some resources that will enable you to follow up on those issues of greatest important to your particular work.

It is our hope that the following pages will support you, the researcher, with the technical information you need to utilize the various technologies we discuss in your research endeavors. We wish you the best in your research, and hope you find the resources you seek as you flip through the following pages.

2 DESIGNING AN ONLINE STUDY

Chapter summary

- Conceptualizing and operationalizing a study
- Questions related to method selection
- Sampling
- Selecting a technology
- Service Level Agreements (SLAs)

Getting started and conceptualizing

Like any other research endeavor, online research begins with interests and ideas and various theoretical perspectives that inform the development of a project. Before thinking through technological issues and challenges for a given study, researchers should spend time working through the specifics of their research endeavor. The types of issues include project timing, clarity of the research problem to be studied, objectives for the research, activities and methodologies to be undertaken in the research, anticipated outcomes and, when appropriate, available funding. Of course, none of this is new to a researcher.

Where online research begins to deviate from traditional research is in conceptualizing and operationalizing the research endeavor. Meanings can be slightly different and nuanced in online environments. Mann and Stewart state: "CMC has characteristics which do not fit within more traditional modes of data collection and which may challenge some standard assumptions about language use, interpersonal relationship and group dynamics" (2000: 3). As such, care should be taken in conceptualizing the research effort so that all language and core constructs are clearly defined and understood. For example, "flaming" can be an adjective describing something that is on fire, in American culture it can be descriptive slang for a homosexual male perceived to be flaunting his sexuality, and online it refers to posting hostile or insulting messages. These different meanings illustrate the need for clarity in language used in online research.

Some social scientists study group dynamics. The research methods of interviewing and focus groups often depend on interpersonal dynamics. While the online environment offers opportunities, it also presents challenges for an interviewer or a focus group moderator. For example, in the context of a focus group, people often express a feeling of being in a bubble. They know a researcher is evaluating the group dynamics. But they also note that it's one thing to see the two-way mirror in the research lab and know someone is watching, and yet another not to see anything but have the feeling that you're being watched in a study.

Another group dynamic challenge for a researcher managing an online focus group is the fact that it's possible to recruit participants from a wide range of cultural backgrounds. Understandably, most welcome the richness that will come from the data. However, few will consider the fact that participants coming from different cultural perspectives may require more work in facilitating a group dynamic. Once a group interacts well together, there can be a greater emphasis on the point of view of the participants rather than the researcher's perspective, limiting researcher bias. With that benefit, however, comes the potential for the researcher to lose some control of the discussion, creating management challenges. Another challenge for researchers is the potential for participants in an interview or a focus group to respond or send an additional response before receiving or reading a previous message. This can complicate the management of discussion threads and can lead the discussion into a different direction. It can also be awkward for participants, who may not know how to re-enter a discussion that has shifted into two different directions (Gaiser, 2000). These are issues that should be considered as your research is being designed.

Operationalizing a research study refers to the concrete steps or operations that will be used to measure specific concepts (Babbie, 2007). At this stage in research design, the challenge is to determine the best ways in which to attack a research question. The researcher needs to determine what has to be illuminated and in what ways the research should be conducted. Ultimately, operationalizing a project should lead to clarity regarding data collection.

Tips 'n Tricks

Guidelines
Think a study through from beginning to ending

- Think through the research goals.
- Choose a research method.
- Analyze the methodological challenges and issues (legal requirements, issues of privacy, etc.).
- Determine an appropriate technology to meet your research needs.
- Think through your implementation of the technology, including any analysis needs.
- Think through your implementation of the overall study.

As you begin to formulate your study, it's useful to keep a few general thoughts in mind. Online it is tempting for people to think they are playing a game; many people interact online as a form of entertainment. As Busiel and Maeglin (1998) point out, it's easy to lose sight of your purpose. They also note that it's easy to get lost in a vast amount of information. The internet has massive stores of data which grow incrementally each day. It's easy to become overwhelmed or simply to use the first thing you find, whether or not it's the best resource for your particular purposes. In some cases, there can be a learning curve for both the researcher and the participant. Throughout this book, we will recommend basic technologies and advice for easing the learning curve. Finally, while technology is changing the face of the planet, there still is a digital divide and, unfortunately, the online environment still reflects the socio-economic and other realities of society. All of these issues will have some impact on the decisions you make as you begin to develop and conduct an online study, and so will be discussed in the following pages.

Who is researching what online?

In the early 1990s, it was difficult to find an online study that had been published. Today, there are a number of studies and books in various disciplines that provide some guidance as to what might constitute an online study. Communication theorists, for example, have focused on the linguistic status and characteristics of forms of computer-mediated communication (Davis & Brewer, 1997; Herring, 1996). Some social theorists focus on the impact of computer-mediated communication on social interactions and the presentation of self online (Hine, 2000; Turkle, 1995). Others focus on the cultural anthropology of the environment and the impact of that culture on daily life, if any (Rheingold, 1995; Turkle, 1993). Educational researchers are interested in knowing what role the internet plays in education, the quality of internet-based educational models, the specifics of the delivery of education online, and the shifting roles of teacher/trainer and learner (Coiro, Knobel, Lankshear & Leu 2008; Comeaux, 2005).

Many studies have come from the discipline of psychology and have been conducted in a controlled environment (Dubrovsky, Kiesler & Sethna 1991; Weisband, Schneider & Connolly 1992), evaluating whether or not computer-mediated environments provide an equalizing effect on status levels for participants. Many have also been in relation to employment issues (Bishop, 1993; Forester, 1992; Rifkin, 1995; Zuboff, 1988), focusing on organizational concerns, worker autonomy and the transformation of social relations in the workplace. Some have also focused on gender differences, or the lack thereof, both in acquiring technological knowledge (Zubrow, 1989) and in using computer technology (Nassr-Charlebois, 1990). Research has varied method-ologically, with many studies being quantitative (Kraft, 1987; Walther, Anderson & Park, 1994) and others being qualitative in the ethnographic tra-dition (Clodius, 1994; Turkle, 1995; Zubrow, 1989). Sherry Turkle, for exam-ple, on the Massachusetts Institute of Technology faculty, conducts interviews with participants, looking at the psychological implications of the infusion of computers into our daily lives. In particular, Turkle's work pursues the rela-tionship between our interactions with computers and the ways in which we perceive our sense of self. In her early work, she examines how information technology affords individuals an opportunity for reflection, suggesting it pro-vides a lens through which we can reconsider ourselves, hence a "second" self (1984). In later work, Turkle highlights the ways in which individuals recon-struct their identities to participate in a computerized culture, both on and off the screen. She describes "how a nascent culture of simulation is affecting our ideas about mind, body, self, and machine" (1995: 10). In her work, she sug-gests that the computer not only provides an opportunity for users to reflect, but also provides opportunities for people to reconstruct their identity.

Other researchers have analyzed and evaluated interactions and issues regarding the way people communicate online in an attempt to move toward an understanding of what might be conceived of as a community. Steven Jones edited a collection of essays focused on assisting "its readers to become aware and critical of the hopes we have pinned on computer-mediated communica-tion and of the cultures that are emerging among network users" (1995). Participant experiences of online group activity have been analyzed against a typology of various communal forms to illuminate an understanding of what might be referred to as the social form of online community (Gaiser, 2000).

There have been a number of books and papers written on the subject of emerging communities enabled by computer-mediated communication. Some of the literature is case-study oriented (Rheingold, 1993; Smith, 1992), while other publications are anthologies that begin the search for new social forms in cyberspace and raise sociological questions regarding their nature (Jones, 1995). As noted by Jones, "Just because the spaces with which we are now concerned are electronic is not the case that they are democratic, egalitarian, or accessible, and it is not the case that we can forego asking in particular about substance and dominance" (1995: 23). Like other social scientists, Jones raises questions about these new social forms online and calls for researchers to evaluate them.

In education, researchers are attempting to expand educational models beyond the standard modes of assessment. In an assessment of online educational venues, the lines between learning and evaluation are often blurred, where the focus is on the creation of knowledge (Burnett & Roberts, 2005: 55–6). The threaded discussions, or rather, chronological listing of participants comments, employed by Burnett and Roberts in their research with Australian undergraduates function as a type of unmoderated focus group. In this case, the group was given some orientation statements and a task. They collectively produced knowledge in the form of a new "guiding principle model" for teacher education (Burnett & Roberts, 2005: 58).

Selecting a method (from a technological vantage point)

Understandably, a method is determined by the nature of the research project and the specific questions that will be addressed in the study. Some considerations reflect potential legal challenges, such as those pertaining to an individual's privacy. In the United States, the Health Insurance Portability and Accountability Act (HIPAA) regulates how private details about an individual are to be protected. For example, someone designing an online study that looks at mental health issues, should take note of HIPAA regulations prior to beginning the research. The kinds of questions that might need to be considered include:

• Can participant security be guaranteed? Anonymity? Protection of the data?
• Can someone ever really be anonymous online? And if not, how might this impact the overall study design?
• Can someone "see" a participant's information when s/he participates?
• Can someone unassociated with the study access data on a hard drive?
• Should there be an informed consent to participate? If so, how might online security issues impact the informed consent?
• If a study design calls for participant observation, is it okay to "lurk"? Is it always okay? If not, then when? What are the determining factors?
• Is it okay to deceive online? What constitutes online deception?

These types of questions will impact the specifics of a chosen method and how it is implemented online. For example, IP (internet protocol) addresses can be tracked, providing information about a user by identifying the source of a given email. Thus, some might argue that it is impossible to "guarantee" anonymity or participant security. That is not to say that reasonable precautions and attempts cannot be made, as are outlined in the following pages, but rather to indicate that an honest, informed consent form should provide some specific details regarding the issues and how the researcher will attempt to address them. This knowledge might impact the online method, for example, in that a synchronous chat might be selected over the asynchronous method of email participation in a listserv discussion, to maximize control of the content and limit exchanges of information via potentially unsecured email channels.

Similarly, it is important to consider who you want to participate in your study. Some adults might be excluded in a study, because of limited access to a chat room, while young people might be prevented from participating because of parental controls set on a computer.

Tips 'n Tricks

Questions to ask when considering sampling

- Who is online?
- How do you reach a certain population of participants?
- How do you attain a random sample?
- Does it matter who participates?
- Will you want to collect demographic details?
- How will you recruit participants?; "What's in it for them?"

Many of us in the United States can recall the incorrect poll findings of the Literary Digest that predicted that Alf Landon would defeat President Roosevelt in 1936 (Squire, 1988) and the Gallup Polls of 1948 that predicted Thomas Dewey's win over the incumbent Harry S. Truman (http://www.loc.gov/exhibits/treasurestrm 145.html accessed on 21 March 2007). In each case, the samples were skewed by the over-inclusion of wealthy individuals. To use an online example as an illustration, it is unlikely that an online study of society's readiness to accept, and adapt to, a new technology will yield accurate results, as a disproportionate number of individuals online are likely to be more willing to accept a new technology than the general population. The point is that not every study is appropriate for the online environment, for any number of reasons. In addition, there may be specific challenges that need to be recognized regarding accessing a particular population before designing a study.

There are a number of issues to consider when thinking about a research sample for any study. Designing an online study simply compounds the questions and issues. Consider who you want in the study and where you are going to find them. Who is likely to frequent your type of online environment? How can you get participants to participate in your site? How might a researcher best engage a particular population? What technologies do sample participants use, or are more likely to use? So, for example, if the goal is to reach a young, technology savvied population likely to pursue high-tech jobs, then game rooms and gaming interactive technologies are a likely place to start pursuing research participants. These are the types of issues regarding sampling that need to be considered prior to designing the technique for data collection.

Selecting a technology or technologies

After determining what kinds of challenges are most crucial in the research design, the next question is which technologies will enable you, the researcher, to complete the tasks at hand while also addressing your research concerns and challenges.

Tips 'n Tricks

Typical questions to consider regarding your choice of technology

- What is most appropriate to my particular research need?
- What will facilitate and ease the process of data analysis?
- What will be easy to use and develop for research purposes?
- What will be easy for participants to use?
- What will be most cost effective (what's the cost/benefit analysis)?

In selecting a technology, advertising and the hottest trends are typically unhelpful and even, possibly, unreliable. Technical support staff within your organization will know all of the most exciting and cutting-edge technologies, but will often lack the sophistication to understand data-analysis needs or be able to help in thinking through a researcher's particular needs. For example, when it became widely known that FileMaker Pro could be used to develop an online survey, faculty members at our university would often consider using it to enhance their research. There would be initial excitement generated by support staff about the supposed "ease of use" and the faculty members' deep desire to enter the realm of online research. Few, however, considered the fact that they had to learn how to configure the application (or hire someone, most often a research assistant), and develop the survey instrument using the application. Few researchers took the time to think through the ramifications of technical support and the need for a server to "host" the survey. Once a faculty member realized that someone needed the technical skills, and/or aptitude, to develop the research instrument using the application, manage data collection, provide technical support to users, and host the application and survey on a server (including all of the issues related to managing through a firewall, etc.), reality inevitably set in.

In some cases, faculty members would be excited about finding and funding a top-notch graduate assistant, who would diligently produce a very fashionable survey instrument, writing useful macros for data management and download, only to discover that students, being transient, were unable to sustain the research efforts after graduation.

Technologies evolve. Technical support can be expensive. New technologies are developed every day. Often basic technologies can meet a specific need. For these reasons and more, it's important to think through a wide range of issues, both technical and non-technical, before embarking on an online study.

Our advice is to do some information gathering and assessment before determining which technology is best for you:

- Speak with colleagues both in and out of your particular field.
- Review what others have done by looking at a variety of publications and online listings:
  - What technology did they use?
  - What challenges did they experience?
  - What do they feel they missed due to their choices?
- Conduct a self-assessment of your own level of technical skill.

Your review of these issues, along with your evaluation of the various available technologies, both as we've outlined in this book as well as elsewhere, should enable you to make an educated and informed decision about which technology is best for you.

To be clear, the preceding comments are not meant to suggest that researchers should relinquish any hope of conducting research online. On the contrary, we offer this book precisely so that you can make educated decisions and get started with ease. The purpose of this text is to help you, the reader, avoid the mistakes we've made or witnessed over the years, and to provide you with some of the practical tips we've learned through experience, so that you have at your disposal what you need to make educated decisions.

Data collection

The reason we develop research instruments is so that we can collect data that will help us develop a new understanding. To that end, when using a technology for data collection, it's important to keep in mind whether or not the technology will facilitate data collection, management and analysis. Some applications, such as mIRC, allow you to create logs as text-only files. These logs are easily identifiable as #yourchannel_160 222007.log (http://www.nic.fi/~mauvinen/mircstats/mircstatsfaq.html#multifiles, accessed 9 April 2007). In addition, you can search through log files, and then prepare them in whatever manner is necessary to access them through an analytical program. For example, using an application like HyperResearch might necessitate separating key sections of the discussion with a tilde (~) to make coding and analysis more manageable. In a given study, there may be statements from different participants that should be separated for coding purposes, or a need to break a file due to changes in the discussion thread or different dates. The point to consider is whether or not data are easily cleaned and analyzed, or whether there are complex steps or translations that need to be completed prior to analysis.

Tips 'n Tricks

Data analysis guidelines
Some general guides to follow when considering
issues of data analysis

- Qualitative data may need to be saved in a **text only** (.txt) or **rich text format** (.rtf) with few extraneous symbols or markings.
- Qualitative data may need to be formatted in a specific way for use in a particular research application (e.g. HyperReseach or NVIVO.
- Quantitative data may need to be "cleaned" so that they contain few, if any, extraneous symbols or markings.
- It may be necessary to be familiar with a spreadsheet application (e.g. Microsoft Excel) to aid simple data cleaning with the ability to search, cut and paste.

Supporting the research participant

Too often when preparing to conduct an online study, researchers focus on their own needs and issues of ease of use and neglect the needs of participants. For example, a market researcher may consider conducting a focus group using a shareware chat application to conduct a study with a group of corporate clients. While focusing on logging capabilities and ease of management for conducting the focus group, the marketer may neglect to consider that some corporate policies will not allow staff to download applications on a company computer. Others may have firewalls configured to prevent an individual from participating in a chat session. In other cases, participants may have limited, if any, technical skills, requiring the researcher to do a great deal of virtual hand-holding to facilitate their participation. In the end, assuming the study proceeds, it may be more prudent to consider these types of user issues prior to embarking on a study.

The technical cost/benefit analysis

If money were no object, everyone would have access to a variety of technical tools and ample technical support. Alas, however, this is not the case, particularly in academia. Therefore, a researcher needs to consider a cost/benefit analysis when investing in a research study. When conducting self-administered, mail-in surveys, most people know how to budget. In most cases, researchers know the going rate for a research assistant and can determine the time it takes to administer a questionnaire. Generally, using technological solutions will prove to be considerably less expensive than more traditional methods. However, a mistake or poor investment can also be quite costly. For example, it probably doesn't make sense to buy a server ($2,000), install the necessary system and application software ($2,000), and pay for management of the server (@ $25–$75/hr) to run a basic survey when it would be much more cost effective to create a simple survey instrument that can be emailed or one using an online service such as Survey Monkey (www.surveymonkey.com).

Tips 'n Tricks

AVOIDING EXPENSIVE MISTAKES
Types of mistakes that can derail a study and/or lead to considerable expense

Mistake #1

... **allowing an energetic and technically savvied assistant to write a unique program for your research that becomes central to your data-collection efforts.** If the program stops working after your assistant has graduated or taken a different position and moved on, having to change your technology in mid-study or, worse, having to pay a professional programmer to reverse-engineer your application or fix it can be extremely expensive.

Mistake #2

... **becoming dependent on an expensive and complex application that requires advanced-level skills that are costly to access in the open market.** A colleague might be right that an Oracle database is the most robust, or MySQL makes for a great online survey ... but Oracle and SQL programmers often command a high salary in the job market, and database programming, SQL server management, etc., all tend to cost money. Again, you may have a colleague or high-end assistant now, but what happens when they are no longer available to you?

Mistake #3

... **using the first application that appears to meet an immediate need without thinking through all the relevant issues specific to a given study.** A particular application recommended by one of your assistants or a colleague may be a good place to start your research preparation. But it is little use to you if the functions needed are inadequate or non-existent. Begin with the advice of others, but proceed by thinking through your specific needs *before* pursuing the use of a recommended technology.

When thought through carefully, technological solutions for online research can be highly cost effective. Often, return rates are as high if not higher than traditional mailed surveys, there are no costs for transcription or data entry, and many research applications are freeware, shareware or relatively inexpensive. Applications that are purchased have a useful life beyond any given study and can usually be upgraded for a fraction of the original cost.

Highlighting the potential for costly mistakes is not meant to dissuade you from venturing into technological waters, but rather to encourage you to pause and reflect, with the information we've provided, so that, ultimately, your experience can be more productive.

Service Level Agreements (SLAs) ... "I don't know what I don't know"

A service level agreement is one of those things few know anything about, or even know that it's worth knowing anything about. If you accept that there are times when you "don't know what you don't know," then we encourage you to read on. This is probably one of those occasions.

What is a service level agreement (SLA)? Isn't that a business thing? Well, yes ... and also no. An SLA is an agreement that makes explicit the expectations of two parties, formally defining a certain level of service. A formal SLA is most often found in business arrangements. For example, a bank that receives technical services for its online banking through an outside vendor would have, as part of its overall contract, an SLA that defines the specifics of its relationship with the vendor.

So then why is an SLA discussed here? Why should someone who isn't working in a corporate environment care about an SLA? The most direct answer to that question is that anyone who deals with anyone else to support their research efforts should consider having some type of SLA. You may be a market researcher using one of your business servers (whether in-house or externally) to host a chat and store data. You probably have a technical support person, who is probably a jack of all trades when it comes to technical matters, who has been happy to help with set-up, installing software, configuring applications, etc. Then one day your application crashes in the middle of heavy use. You have focus groups scheduled. You panic, because things aren't working correctly. You call your technical support person for assistance, and he replies that he needs to finish installing the updated version of Windows on a colleague's computer before he deals with your server issue. To you, it's a crisis. To him, it's another task on a long list. Negotiating an SLA prior to embarking on your study will help manage the expectations of both of you. You will have a clear sense of what you can expect for support, and he will have agreed to some level of priority for your technical needs.

We once supported a researcher in developing an online survey. Although online survey services were available to her, she decided it was better to develop her own tool on local systems. She had concerns about security and also had a more complicated survey instrument than the average online service could provide … at least, that was the case at that time. We had little trouble developing the instruments, because there were ample techies at our disposal willing to do the development work for her interesting and challenging research instrument. Over a short period of time, various surveys became active, data collection commenced, and she was very happy with her research project. One evening, during part of a routine system back-up, everything came crashing down. All of the instruments went off-line and required manual restarts. All were in locked server rooms, on servers with administrator pass-words that were unknown to her or any of the survey developers. When she was finally able to track down the system administrator, she was reminded that everything in the organization had gone down and her surveys weren't top priority. While she has continued to use the survey services and has worked with the same support personnel for other projects, from that point forward she has negotiated an SLA for every project.

When conducting an online study, part of the process of preparation should include creating an SLA. In most cases, the researcher will not be hosting his or her own research instrument or research environment. In some cases, such as with an online chat tool, services may be web based and widely available. In other cases, such as in the development of a survey instrument, if not using an online service then hosting will likely be on a locally managed server. If the server is not owned, operated and actively managed by the research team, an SLA is warranted.

Essentially, an SLA is an arrangement between two parties with regard to a provided service. In the technical world, an SLA is a contract between a customer and a service provider. Although this may sound a bit formal for agreements within an organization, which it is, it's still an optimal way to ensure proper support. Given that technical staff are rarely, if ever, dedicated to a particular project, their obligations and commitments are divided between a number of customers. Therefore, which priority should the research project be? Should it be first, because the researcher thinks his/her work takes precedent? Should it be second, because research isn't the top priority of the rest of the institution? The point is that an SLA enables everyone to develop shared understandings and be clear on expectation, something that's prudent and beneficial in any relationship.

Tips 'n Tricks

Elements of a Service Level Agreement (SLA)

- Identify and define your needs.
- Provide a framework for shared understanding.
- Simplify complex issues.
- Reduce potential areas of conflict.
- Encourage dialog in the event of disputes.
- Eliminate unrealistic expectations.

Source: The Service Level Agreement Zone (http://www.sla-zone.co.uk), accessed on 9 April 2007

An SLA should embrace a wide range of issues. The most immediate and obvious issue pertains to what services are to be provided. Do services include data back-up and at what intervals (daily, weekly, monthly)? In the event of system failure, at what priority level will a survey instrument be restored? Who, specifically, is responsible? If you are using an application that requires a manual restart, who is responsible for restarting the research instrument? If and when the server requires routine maintenance, how will maintenance be planned, scheduled and communicated and who will be responsible for doing each step? Likewise, if the application being used for research requires an update, what is the process for acquiring the update and installing it? Who is responsible for performing application updates, including any necessary testing to ensure the system is fully operational after installation?

Researchers often fail to consider issues like tracking, reporting and performance until they are engaged in the research effort. It is easy to be focused on operationalizing a study and not thinking about the technical details. Then, as the study commences, the researcher begins to ask questions such as, "How many people have accessed my site?" and "Is it possible for me to determine how long it takes people to complete my survey?" These, and others, are useful questions. But it is important to keep in mind that, as noted previously, many technical employees have other obligations. They have better things to do than spend time accessing system statistics for one individual. It might be possible to automate some of these statistics so that the research team can access regular reports. It might also be something that can be included in the tasks of the technical staff, if negotiated up front. Although the kinds of things needed may not be known until the study gets under way, it is useful to include some general thoughts on performance statistics when crafting the SLA.

Working hard to develop a shared understanding of the research project and mutual expectations does not, necessarily, imply that a project will be conflict-free. A good agreement includes a process for addressing conflict and dispute resolution. It may be jointly understood that any system updates will be purchased and installed by the technical staff. An update is announced which the research team thinks it's necessary to install, as it is supposed to enhance a certain kind of functionality related to the research effort. The system staff, however, feel the update is unwarranted and have chosen not to make the purchase. How does this dispute get resolved? Who has final authority? While a good SLA limits the likelihood of any major conflict, it is advisable to think through how conflict will be handled before an occasion presents itself. Clarity regarding conflict resolution can mitigate loss of active research time while resolving a dispute.

Routine maintenance and obligations should be spelled out clearly. Who runs regular back-ups? Do system back-ups cover data back-ups or does the research team need to routinely run their own data back-ups? When system patches and updates need to be installed, who is responsible? Does the research team install application patches and the system staff install operating system updates? Does the research team have administrative access to the server? The point is that all duties and responsibilities need to be clearly identified and assigned in the SLA to limit confusion when potential issues arise.

Today people are highly sensitized to issues of privacy and security. Thus, a service level agreement needs to include system security. This information is likely to be necessary for funders and any institutional or professional review boards that evaluate research proposals. Issues related to other operations on the same server, institutional firewalls, and so forth, should all be included and considered. For example, depending on how an institutional firewall is configured, some research operations may be running outside of its confines. It may have been easier for the developer to jump the firewall while configuring an application than to go through the process of seeking permission to run a research project. While the intention was to get a project expeditiously on track, this could be a problem in the long term. Essentially, it could mean that while the front door is bolted shut, the back door has been left wide open. A savvied hacker would be able to find and exploit this security lapse. As such, an SLA should list any and all issues related to security, what steps have been taken to ensure security, and how any security breach will be handled. You should include what you, the researcher, will do as well as what you expect of anyone serving as your technical support. Although the handling of a security breach may seem minor, if an institution's policy is to shut down anything and everything first, and then take its time resolving a problem, this situation could leave your research project offline for many days. This can be considerably frustrating if the researcher has limited knowledge of the problem and considers the problem a minor issue. Therefore, it is advisable to have clarity regarding security issues prior to embarking on a study.

In addition to traditional issues of security, there is a need to be clear on intellectual property rights and any confidential information related to a research project. SLAs should clearly indicate whether or not any information accessible to technical staff is confidential. In addition, anything that would be considered intellectual property should also be clearly spelled out in any agreement. This may seem extreme, but it limits the likelihood of research ideas appearing in an unauthorized blog or web site, or your customized research application, developed with your professional insights, being sold on the open market.

Another area that is often neglected and needs to be clearly spelled out is the lifecycle of a study. When does the study end? How long will the system need to be available to the research staff? What should be the process for terminating the project? What final documentation, disks, files, etc., should be provided to the research team at the conclusion of the project? It is considerably frustrating for technical staff to be left wondering about the answers to these questions. Likewise, it can be a source of frustration for a researcher to experience pressure to make decisions s/he is unprepared to make. These issues should be considered and clearly defined prior to the start of a study. It is fine for a study to have a long life. What is important is that everyone understands milestones, how and when decisions will be made about the continued life of a study, when those decisions will be made, and by whom.

A final note on SLAs. Nothing needs to be written in stone. The purpose of the SLA is to give people the means for dialog and shared expectations. Research needs change. System operations change. Staffing needs change. With a working document, these changes can be easily addressed without creating any complications for the overall project or people involved. (A good reference for service level agreements is http://www.sla-zone.co.uk which was accessed on 9 April 2007.)

The preceding pages are designed to help a researcher address technical issues early in the study design process. As previously stated, the intention is not to deter researchers from embarking on an online research project, or to make the issues appear insurmountable, but rather to enable researchers to be more efficient and knowledgeable as they move forward in their research design. The following chapter will build upon the issues raised in this chapter by offering additional challenges, unique to the online environment, for consideration; and some practical ways in which to address them.

3 RESEARCH STANDARDS AND ETHICAL CONSIDERATIONS

Chapter summary

- Research standards
- Ethical considerations
- Informed consent
- Confidentiality and anonymity

Research standards

All disciplines have some kind of research standard to which practitioners are expected to adhere. As a general rule, the research standards in a given discipline are where a researcher should begin their own review for a new research endeavor. All research standards have some type of expectation for ethical standards. Others, like medical disciplines such as nursing, will have substantive guidelines regarding the protection of participants, with an expectation of privacy that protects an individual's identity as well as the information they provide in a study. In a discipline such as marketing, the Market Research Association provides standards regarding the use of push technologies and manipulative pseudo-sales practices (http://www.mra-net.org/pdf/expanded_code.pdf, accessed on 10 May 2007). In others, such as the American Sociological Association, the Code of Ethics clearly states that a researcher should avoid a conflict of interest by not seeking to gain from information accessed through the research effort (http://www.asanet.org/page.ww?section=Ethics&name=Code+of+Ethics+Stand ards#9, accessed on10 May 2007).

Typical research standards will provide guidance on issues such as:

- sampling
- participant protection/informed consent
- data acquisition
- data management
- conflict of interest.

While a number of topics will be discussed in the following section relating to the unique issues presented by online research, readers are encouraged to review the research standards in a given discipline before embarking on a research project. A list of some potential sources follows:

http://onlineethics.org/reseth/index.html (engineering)
http://www.mra-net.org/pdf/expanded_code.pdf (marketing)
http://www.asanet.org/cs/root/leftnav/ethics/code_of_ethics_table_of_contents (sociology)
http://www.apa.org/science/standards.html (educational testing)
http://www.srcd.org/ethicalstandards.html (child development)
http://www.ethicsweb.ca/resources/research/ (collective listing)

Tips 'n Tricks

Guidelines

- Review discipline-specific guidelines.
- Note the types of questions researchers might want to ask themselves.
- Consider the types of questions that might arise from your chosen method in a review process.
- Think like a funder or review board and consider what reviewers might be looking for.
- Identify how you'll address technical questions related to security of data, protection of participants, and so on (data storage, data management, downloading online, file encryption, etc.)

Ethical considerations

At some point in study design, a researcher should spend time evaluating ethical considerations. Many people believe that "ethical" and "legal" are considered one and the same. Researchers, however, know otherwise. There are times when something may be considered legal, such as a study that deploys deception, but the practice may not be considered acceptable in a given discipline. As an illustration, I (TJG) once received an email indicating that I owed the other person several dollars and was probably too drunk at a party the previous evening to realize I had borrowed the money. As I was confident I had not been out the previous night and knew I hadn't borrowed any money, I was intrigued. I did a little sleuthing and discovered that someone in the Psychology Department was conducting a study on people's reactions to email and was sending out messages to a random group of individuals on the university system to determine how people would react to a provocative and inaccurate email. In this instance, deception was necessary to evoke a response. If the researcher's discipline had frowned upon this type of deception for research purposes, the researcher would have needed to rethink the purpose and design of the study.

While traditional research ethics are a useful starting point, the online environment represents new ethical challenges for researchers that require thinking outside of the boundaries of traditional research. Informed consent, confidentiality, anonymity, privacy, the nature of what constitutes private and public spaces, virtual personae, copyright, and more, take on new meanings and require fresh insights when you are conducting research in the online environment.

Most online methods books will include comments on the topic of ethical challenges, such as Annette Markham's (1998) discussion about being honest about her age online, or Christine Hine's (2000) discussion of self-disclosure – or not – as an active participant/researcher in an online newsgroup. In addition, there are articles such as Susannah Stern's in *New Media & Society* (2003) and books such as Elizabeth Buchanan's *Readings in Virtual Research Ethics: Issues and Controversies* (2004) that offer fresh and helpful insights. Online researchers are well advised to venture into the emerging literature to review ethical considerations as they design and pursue an online study.

Data storage

In the past, technological innovations have raised new methodological questions on conducting research. For example, taped interviews raised questions of who would have access to the tape, where it would be stored, and who would be responsible for making those decisions. Likewise, video cameras raised many similar issues (Shrader-Frechette, 1994; Sieber, 1992). Researchers turned to the guidelines of their respective professions seeking hints and advice so they could make judgments about these issues relative to their research. Similarly, many would like to be responsible about respecting the privacy and confidentiality of research subjects in cyberspace. However, the technology of computer-mediated communication raises issues that have not been dealt with in previous research. Lacking satisfactory encryption, for example, can a researcher guarantee participant protection of privacy and confidentiality (Eisenberg, 1996)?

Due to the way in which messages are relayed back and forth across the internet, there are many ways that they can remain on a remote server somewhere. Lacking sufficient ability to track tapping, unlike telephone research where tapping is quite easily noted, can researchers be sure no one else is reading the discussion (Flower, 1994)? The point is that with past technologies the researcher had a physical audio tape, transcript, video tape, etc., that was filed and maintained in spaces they controlled (Sieber, 1992). But with computer-mediated communication, the researcher has much less control over the data. Encryption and security have not attained levels whereby anyone on the internet could legitimately guarantee a volunteer's privacy and/or confidentiality. When a volunteer is recruited for an online focus group or interview, the individual is being asked to be exposed to some level of risk that a researcher has little to no control over. Text is often retrievable even when it was not intentionally archived. Those with the technological knowledge and interest will have access to a great deal of information about the participant, whether or not the researcher provides permission.

The Rimm study provides an illustration of the debate regarding the use of online data. Marty Rimm was a student at Carnegie-Mellon, and the principal investigator in a study of internet pornography entitled "Marketing Pornography on the Information Superhighway" (http://TRFN.pgh.pa.us/guest/mrtext.html). Since publication of the study in the *Georgetown Law Journal* and subsequent press coverage, there has been debate about issues of privacy and what constitutes "ethical" methods in online research. One critique of the research claimed Rimm failed to protect the anonymity of those studied and deceived participants (http://www2000.ogsm.vanderbilt.edu/cyberporn.debate.cgi). The charges stem from the fact that Rimm accessed server information on people who had no idea they were participants. Furthermore, he shared the data without making an attempt to strip it of any traceable identity. The net result was that two individuals were prosecuted and went to prison, due, arguably, to the publication of the study. While one could debate whether or not they deserved to go to prison, the reality still remains that they were not informed of their participation in a research study and data from the study led to imprisonment.

The complexity of computer-mediated communication requires researchers to utilize available guides when determining what constitutes acceptable practice in their own fields of research, prior to embarking on a major online study. Professional organizations have developed guidelines to enable people to address a variety of concerns in the design of their research. In many instances, it is sufficient to demonstrate respect for the rights and welfare of participants (Diener & Crandell, 1978; Reynolds, 1982). There are times, of course, when researchers will have to weigh the respect for individual rights against the overall benefit to society. But as there are no clear answers, researchers need to demonstrate they have weighed the factors and considered the consequences of their research and the welfare of those affected. Researchers need to ask themselves whether they can protect participants in online research, and whether the answer to this question limits their options for conducting research in this environment. Therefore, before beginning a project, the ethical implications of a project need to be carefully considered.

Copyright and identification

In many online discussion lists dominated by academic researchers, a number of discussions have focused on the issue of whether or not electronic correspondence and various server log files and archives represent public data. Some researchers have maintained that because no one has established clear guidelines for conducting online research, anything is fair game. On the topic of legality, most discussions have the tendency to conclude that if it is not illegal, it is ethical. For many, the lack of codified etiquette and guidelines for conducting research in cyberspace makes most anything permissible.

Unique to the online environment is the question of "publicly" available data. Is someone's participation in a chat room or on a blog considered publicly available data? Are log files public? Are user statistics collected by a host server public data? Who owns a posting to a discussion list? Is it the person who posted the message? Is it the owner of the discussion list (the moderator)? If the message was posted with the inclusion of the initial message text to another discussion group, who owns it then? As Mann and Stewart note, some hold that any type of quoting necessitates crediting the source (2000: 45). Otherwise, use of the data is a violation of copyright. Another perspective is that when we read something that wasn't sent to us or something in a discussion group that is a response to a particular individual's posting, we are, so to speak, overhearing someone else's conversation (Lawson, 2004: 90). You didn't solicit the communication, nor do you have any direct claim over its content.

It's important to note that when considering the legal limits of copyright protection in the online environment, there are two aspects of copyright licensing that may apply: implied license and fair use. Neither has been exhausted in the courts, so specifics may change with time. Many people would consider using textual data from an online discussion as constituting "fair use." The logic would be that since quotations from a speech, address or position paper in a news report are considered fair use, then a contribution to an online discussion would be the equivalent of a public address (http://www.bitlaw.com/copyright/fair_use.html accessed on 10 April 2008). One caveat in this approach, though, is that online the data are actual text and not a verbal message. The fact that these are in textual form may one day lead to a legal challenge to that understanding.

Similarly, some have noted "implied license" within copyright law (Mann & Stewart, 2000: 46; http://www.bitlaw.com/copyright/license.html accessed 10 April 2008). Since sending a message online implies the intention for others to read and save it, there is an implied license. Mann and Stewart suggest that some would distinguish between private and semi-private communication and publicly accessed communication. In the case of intentional interaction (private and semi-private communication), informed consent precedes the use of data, governing the ways in which the data can and should be used (2000: 46).

While concern for copyright and ownership of a participant's words may appear fairly straightforward to some, as Lawson (2004: 90) notes,

> crediting CMC (computer-mediated communication) texts used in academic publications to the participant who authored the texts raises another ethical dilemma for researchers, who must now decide which is more important, giving participants credit for their intellectual property in the form of CMC written communication or protecting their identities and anonymity as participants of the research in question.

Statements attributed to a participant in a business study about an employment environment could cost an employee his or her job. Statements about sexuality or alternative lifestyles could damage an individual's reputation or, at the very least, prove to be embarrassing.

There is no hard and fast rule as to whether it is ethical to access and use data from a site, outside of attributing authorship where it is due. Some researchers refrain from using any data not provided specifically for their research, while others use whatever they find. As a general rule, it is a good idea – particularly when entering an online community – to interact with a site moderator/creator/manager about the research effort, how participants will be approached, how the research will be presented to participants, and how data will be collected and used. In addition, Lawson (2004: 91) offers the following thoughts for protecting a participant's identity:

- Use disguises for names and communities.
- Delete or mask compromising details as much as possible.
- Create composite characters.
- Break identifiable characters into multiple characters to make them less identifiable.

While these rules are not foolproof, they allow for the use of data when the issue is less about copyright and more about protecting the privacy and identity of a participant. It should be noted that disguises and changed identity can also have an impact on the presentation of findings. If a name is changed, for example, it could impact meaning (Maczewski, Storey & Hoskins 2004). Maybe a participant has the username of Bilbo21. By changing that name, the meaning of a hobbit-related joke in the discourse would be lost. We often don't realize that type of significance until we conduct our analysis. So it is necessary to consider the potential significance of this type of lost meaning as you design a study and negotiate the informed consent process with participants.

One of the things a researcher is doing when engaging in an informed consent process is establishing trust between the researcher and the participant. One of the ways of improving the odds of accessing quality information, or, more specifically, getting participants to give in-depth, honest answers to questions, is to help a participant be confident that he or she can trust the researcher to do what he or she says they will do. Unfortunately, that task is confounded by the fact that just as other people on the internet can create new identities online, so, too, can the researcher. This ability of the researcher to create an alternative identity can present a problem in the establishment of trust (Maczewski et al., 2004: 71).

Not only is the establishment of trust compromised by the possibility that a researcher may not be who he or she says, but it can also be confounded by the basics of one's self-presentation. Lacking all of the usual visual and vocal cues for self-presentation (Goffman, 1959), online we only have words, word choices, signature files, our email address, and so forth. These are the things that constitute our 'voice' online. Thus, everyone has a certain 'voice' online that may or may not match their voice in real-life encounters. People respond to us based on that online voice (Maczewski et al., 2004).

At one point during a research study on an online community, a participant from Australia telephoned me (TJG). He said that he was interested in speaking with me to see if his perception of my online persona matched what he thought he would learn from a synchronous conversation where he would hear my voice. His impressions of my two personas were not the same. He felt my online presentation was formal, professional and carried an air of intellectual authority (probably a good thing, by the way, since I was the researcher). While he still felt I was articulate in person, to use his words, I also sounded "much younger and sporty than he had initially anticipated." As noted by this encounter, the challenge for researchers is that they need to be aware of their online voice and self-presentation, so as not to have it work against them when attempting to establish trust.

Again, the general point is to be as careful and thoughtful as possible when using data of any kind. Researchers should keep in mind that while they believe a particular piece of data is harmless, others may feel otherwise. At a professional conference, an attendee stated that she felt that her participation in an online forum that was being studied by another colleague impacted her tenure application by identifying her particular intellectual perspective in a way that made her look less desirable to her department. Whether or not it was true or verifiable in any way, the fact remains that she believed it to be true, which should be sufficient reason to give researchers pause for thought.

Informed consent

In any study with research participants, the use of informed consent should be considered. In some cases, a review may lead a researcher to determine that it is not necessary. In other situations, a review will determine that using informed consent is vital. It is worth noting, however, that an informed consent form is useful, if for no other reason than to express a researcher's expectations for the project and the provision of details on the topic being researched. Depending on the study, it can also be an opportunity to explain why the research is being conducted and to provide some autobiographical information about the researcher or research team. Another reason for having an informed consent form is to explain what is expected of participants and to indicate that participating in the research is consider to be giving "consent" to use a participant's responses. In short, the informed consent protects the researcher.

Likewise, informed consent is meant to protect the study participant. Participants may assume and expect that communication is private. They may also have certain expectations about how the data will be used and whether or not their particular words will be used in any publication. Researchers often include statements that indicate that a participant's contribution in their study obliges him or her to protect the participant's biographical anonymity.

The reasons the preceding obligation is important may not always be readily apparent. If study participants are drawn from the internet and include individuals from other cultures, there may be cultural taboos that could impact a participant. For example, if a study includes a discussion about certain sexual activities or inclinations, a particular culture may have taboos that could negatively impact a participant. This problem is compounded by the fact that there is also a kind of perceived anonymity which may lead certain naïve participants to greater self-disclosure. Thus, participants have a tendency to feel their identity is protected and their participation feels like play. This sense of playfulness and protected identity could inadvertently make a participant extremely vulnerable.

The informed consent form provides both the participant and the researcher with a mutual understanding and the opportunity to address at the beginning of the study any questions or concerns unique to a particular project. It also provides a suitable track record in the event of confusion arising at a later point in a project (Nelkin, 1994). For a more extensive discussion of informed consent and related issues, we suggest Mann and Stewart's handbook (2000).

Tips 'n Tricks

Advice for informed consent

- Clarifies the nature of the research and the responsibilities of the investigator prior to conducting the research.
- Uses language that is understandable and respectful of research participants.

- Provides the opportunity to ask questions about any aspect of the research.
- Informs participants of the nature of the research.
- Indicates clearly that participation is voluntary, with a statement that there are no consequences, implied or otherwise, for deciding to withdraw from, or choosing not to participate in, the study.
- Informs participants of any significant factors that may be expected to influence their willingness to participate (e.g. use of personal information, possible risks and benefits of participation, etc.).
- Outlines the nature of confidentiality and how it will or will not be maintained.
- Notes any applicable governmental regulations and, where applicable, institutional review board requirements.

(Adapted from The American Sociological Association's web site, http://www2.asanet.org/members/ecostand2.html accessed 11 April 2007)

Archived data

In addition to being stored by participants, computer-mediated communication may also be archived for later retrieval by others. Text is often retrievable even when it was not intentionally archived. In some instances, text may by read by a search engine even after deletion, making it possible for anyone to retrieve a discussion using a search application such as Google or Yahoo! Hence, there is no such thing as a "private" conversation online. As there are no easy answers, researchers are advised to utilize available guides when determining what constitutes acceptable practice in their own field of research prior to embarking on a major online study.

Unique to the electronic environment is the fact that others can access the research data (Williams, Rice & Rogers, 1988). In this environment, the researcher often cannot control who saves the data nor what is done with it. Although it may not be an issue for others to have access to the data, it should be recognized and acknowledged that by virtue of asking someone to participate in a discussion the researcher is also exposing that individual to a potential misrepresentation of their contribution in someone else's research.

It would be futile and naïve to think that participants in most qualitative research online could be prevented from keeping log files of interactions. In addition, attempting to control it may only drive those storing the data into hiding. Therefore, it is probably best to be open and honest about it. A researcher could indicate that they are aware of the possibility and that they are comfortable with others keeping log files and, possibly, using the data for research purposes. In addition, though, note that a participant, like other researchers, has an ethical obligation to state his or her intentions to others in the group and respect people's wishes if they declined to participate in a "substudy."

Confidentiality and anonymity

Submit "confidentiality and anonymity" in any online search engine and you'll access a wide range of information on the topic. The core issues for online researchers are the secure storage of data and the protection of participant identities.

Anonymity and confidentiality are related online in that a researcher has the option of enabling some level of anonymity to protect confidentiality. Therefore, a decision has to be made as to whether or not participants will have disguised identities in a study, and at what level – high or low – they will be disguised. For example, in a low-disguise situation, a participant in a chat room focus group might use their personal pseudonym or their first name. If a higher level of disguise is sought, personal details of any kind (gender, domain names, institutions, usernames, etc.) would not be used. Researchers are advised to evaluate the guidelines of their discipline as well as review their own study protocol to determine what level of anonymity is appropriate for a given study.

It is important to keep in mind that a desired level of anonymity and a realized level of anonymity may drive technology choices. A researcher may prefer a high level of anonymity with no use of information, such as a participant's institution, that could be tracked. While that may be the hope, using a listserv to conduct a focus group makes that preference extremely difficult, if not unattainable. Many participants may choose to use their work accounts to participate, allowing all other participants to see email addresses, such as user@bc.edu and user@fidelity.com.

The level of anonymity may vary with how data are collected. In the case of blogs, the norm on the internet is that webloggers retain copyright. Thus, there is less need to protect their identity. However, this situation raises a different challenge for the researcher that should be addressed in the informed consent. If a researcher is planning to use content posted to a blog, s/he is obliged to attribute authorship to the blog poster, or make explicit their intentions and how that may differ from normative understandings.

A good strategy for maintaining the anonymity of research participants in a study is to convert any public user identification like names, usernames, IP addresses (e.g. 151.199.48.136), social security numbers or other governmental identification into a unique code. When data are gathered and stored, use the code and not other identifiers. To ensure identity protection, the code for your identifier system should be kept on a separate computer or external disk. In this way, if data are compromised, identities may still be protected.

Issues pertaining to data storage can vary according to technologies available, technologies employed, discipline and even country. There might be requirements for how long data are stored, how these are stored, and who is responsible for storing these. For example, in Australia the Freedom of Information Act suggests that institutions, not researchers, are responsible for long-term data storage. As researchers consider data storage, they should be clear about access being appropriately restricted and also decide on a format that will make it possible to access the data for years to come. In most cases, durability simply implies using the newest storage technology. Current storage options might include an online service, a local data server, a local hard drive, an external hard drive, a removable disk, and a CD or DVD. All options, however, should include a second option as a back-up solution.

Tips 'n tricks

Security tips

- Use passwords that are difficult to break (e.g. a combination of alpha and numeric characters).
- "Portable" also means "easily stolen."
- Be sure file settings don't allow prying eyes.
- Use a unique coding system for participant identifiers.

A basic way to protect a hard drive or personal account is to use password protection. Use combinations of letters and numbers that make sense to you, but are difficult for someone else to guess. For example, you might have a cat named "Boots" and your car license plate number is "CV1779." You could use Boo779ts. Using numbers and letters makes a password difficult to break. The catch is not to use something extremely obvious such as your name and phone number. For example, a name and birthday combination like Jo720hn might not be as secure as other combinations. In addition to using a password, it's important to note that passwords need to be changed periodically. Changing a password approximately every six months is good practice.

If your computer is portable, consider the likelihood that it might get stolen some day. In the past few years, there have been many cases in the news about lost or stolen laptops that contained medical records, credit card information, social security numbers and highly sensitive military information. While no one plans to have their computer stolen, preparing for the possibility is worthwhile. If you must store sensitive data on a portable computer, files should be encrypted.

On a multi-user machine or networked machine, make sure that file permissions are set to prevent unauthorized user access, preventing others from reading or copying files.

Chapter 8, which covers data storage, has some examples on how to encrypt files and also on how to set permissions to restrict access.

In online research, as in other research endeavors, choices and decisions are made that will impact the study and how it will be perceived. It's important that researchers be honest in their description of their research endeavor, work at establishing trust, respect the confidentiality of the research participants, and maintain their promises by only using data as agreed.

In this chapter, our goal was to provide you with a foundation on which to make some of the necessary and perhaps difficult decisions in designing your study. In addition, we offered some practical ways in which a researcher can mitigate the unnecessary risk volunteers are exposed to online by encrypting and restricting access to files. In the following chapters our focus will be more specifically on the ways in which various technologies can be employed to support your online research endeavors.

4 USING EMAIL FOR DATA COLLECTION

Chapter summary

- Overview
- Email clients
- Listservs for group discussions (focus groups)
- Mail storage/management
- Using email for interviewing, focus groups, and surveying

Electronic mail (email) is perhaps the oldest method of computer-based communication and is widely available in one form or another. It can be used for one-to-one, one-to-many and many-to-many communication. In online social research, the use of email has been one of the traditional methods for soliciting and collecting data for studies. Typical uses have been the distribution and collection of surveys, conducting interviews and conducting focus groups. These three roles have distinct needs from email.

- Surveys are formatted text distributed by one sender to multiple recipients. The multiple recipients reply (if they do) to the sender and the interaction ends, though follow-up is possible.
- Interviews consist of an exchange of multiple messages between (usually) two users.
- Focus groups usually take the form of a discussion initiated by a sender with several recipients and may involve many exchanges and possible topic changes.

Before getting into those three topics further, we will describe the various email technologies and email software applications with the aim of considering how they apply to the collection of data.

Email technology background

Email is a "store and forward" technology. Messages are composed by the sender and transmitted to a mail server and, after perhaps several hops, received on the addressee's mail service provider server. The addressee then views from, or retrieves the message to his/her own computer using a mail client (which may be a web browser). Usually, the message remains on the mail server until the user deletes it (or perhaps the service provider deletes it after a certain amount of time, due to policy). Messages may be addressed to a single recipient or multiple recipients. When using email to a group of recipients which is relatively unchanging, or if managing the list of recipients becomes complicated, it is useful to use an email listserver.

These days, email is almost entirely based on internet standards, primarily SMTP (Simple Mail Transport Protocol), so mail from one application can almost always be read with a different application or sent from one type of server to another type. In some cases, a protocol bridge is used to translate between SMTP and a proprietary protocol, for example Lotus/Mail or SoftArc FirstClass. The SMTP standard assumes text-based messages, and in particular assumes the ASCII (American Standard Code for Information Interchange) character codes (essentially the US English alphabet plus digits and a limited selection of punctuation marks). It is possible, however, to transmit other alphabets as well as images and other media by encoding the data as MIME (Multi-purpose Internet Mail Extensions). Most mail applications will handle the encoding when necessary; however there remain a significant number of users with purely text-based email readers, for which these MIME-encoded messages may cause difficulties by being rendered as an unrecognizable encoding rather than the original text.

The SMTP standard details both how the mail servers communicate with each other, and what format the actual mail messages take. Every message begins with several lines that are called the header and contain message metadata. One blank line follows the header, and the rest of the message contains the user content, perhaps encoded. The header lines have a parameter name, followed by a colon, and followed by the value of the parameter. Commonly known parameters are From, To, Date and Subject, with fairly obvious meanings. These are usually displayed by mail clients in or near the message window. Other parameters are less known because they are usually not displayed by default. A few of the important ones (for our purposes) are Return-Path, Message-Id, In-Reply-To and References. The Return-Path describes who will receive a reply to the current message. It is usually the same address as From, but it need not be. There are legitimate reasons for From and Return-Path to be different, but it is also a feature that is abused by scammers. They generate a message that seems to come from a financial institution and has a From address that the user might recognize, but the Return-Path may point to someone trying to harvest user information for malicious purposes. For email exchanges the Message-Id, In-Reply-To and References parameters are important. An example will illustrate: three very short messages follow from an exchange with replies. All are displayed in raw format to show the mail headers. The first is the original message.

```
Return-Path: <schreiner@surfsup.com>
Received: from [] (account schreian@mail.surfsup.com verified) by
fe1.surfsup.com (CommuniGate Pro SMTP 5.1.14) with ESMTPSA id
271155480 for schreiner@surfsup.com; Tue, 25 Mar 2008 13:37:09 -0400
Mime-Version: 1.0 (Apple Message framework v753)
Content-Transfer-Encoding: 7bit
Message-Id: <CE944407-4BF4-4895-8D7A-0D444DFFBE3A@surfsup.com
Content-Type: text/plain; charset=US-ASCII; format=flowed
To: Schreiner Tony <schreiner@surfsup.com>
From: Tony Schreiner <schreiner@surfsup.com>
Subject: message 1
Date: Tue, 25 Mar 2008 13:37:11 -0400
X-Mailer: Apple Mail (2.753)

message 1
```

The parameter to note is Message-Id, which in this case is set to

CE944407-4BF4-4895-8D7A-0D444DFFBE3A@surfsup.com

This is a generated string (nearly) guaranteed to be unique. Next comes a reply to the message.

```
Received: from [] (account schreiner@surfsup.com verified)
  by fe3.surfsup.com (CommuniGate Pro SMTP 5.1.14)
  with ESMTPSA id 265466351 for schreiner@surfsup.com; Tue, 25 Mar
  2008 13:39:45 -0400
Mime-Version: 1.0 (Apple Message framework v753)
In-Reply-To: <CE944407-4BF4-4895-8D7A-0D444DFFBE3A@surfsup.com>
References: <CE944407-4BF4-4895-8D7A-0D444DFFBE3A@surfsup.
com>
Content-Type: text/plain; charset=US-ASCII; format=flowed
Message-Id: <58035CB5-26C2-44AF-8320-CDF01DCA097B@surfsup.
com>
Content-Transfer-Encoding: 7bit
From: Tony Schreiner <schreiner@surfsup.com>
Subject: Re: message 1
Date: Tue, 25 Mar 2008 13:39:49 -0400
To: Tony Schreiner <schreiner@surfsup.com>
```
(Continued)

X-Mailer: Apple Mail (2.753)
On Mar 25, 2008, at 1:37 PM, Tony Schreiner wrote:

> message 1

message 2

Note the Message-Id which has a newly generated ID number, but also a new parameter, In-Reply-To, which has the ID of the original message. Also, in the Subject line is the usual convention of the original subject text but prefaced with Re:. Additionally note that the message includes the original message text prefaced by a ">" character. This is called increasing the quote level. And finally, we show one more message that is a reply to the reply.

Return-Path: <schreiner@surfsup.com>
Received: from [136.167.48.167] (account schreiner@mail.surfsup.com [136.167.48.167] verified)
   by fe2.surfsup.com (CommuniGate Pro SMTP 5.1.14)
   with ESMTPSA id 261948487 for schreiner@surfsup.com; Tue, 25 Mar 2008 13:48:43 -0400
Mime-Version: 1.0 (Apple Message framework v753)
In-Reply-To: <58035CB5-26C2-44AF-8320-CDF01DCA097B@surf sup.com>
References: <CE944407-4BF4-4895-8D7A-0D444DFFBE3A@surf sup.com><58035CB5-26C2-44AF-8320-CDF01DCA097B@ surfsup.com>
Content-Type: text/plain; charset=US-ASCII; format=flowed
Message-Id: <ED243AF1-F92F-4F33-948C-254C4B9D3957@ surfsup.com>
Content-Transfer-Encoding: 7bit
From: Tony Schreiner <schreiner@surfsup.com>
Subject: message3
Date: Tue, 25 Mar 2008 13:48:46 -0400
To: Tony Schreiner <schreiner@surfsup.com>
X-Mailer: Apple Mail (2.753)

On Mar 25, 2008, at 1:39 PM, Tony Schreiner wrote:
> On Mar 25, 2008, at 1:37 PM, Tony Schreiner wrote:
>

```
>> message 1
>
>
> message 2
message 3
```

Note again the Message-Id and In-Reply-To parameters, as well as the new References parameter. The In-Reply-To parameter is message ID of the preceding message, but the References parameter includes all the messages in this exchange (also called a Thread), starting with the original. Just to be different, the Subject line was changed by the sender instead of using the default convention. And note that in the message body the previous message is quoted at level one, while the original message that has made three trips now is quoted at level two. The References parameter helps mail clients sort how message threads are displayed. Even though the subject line was changed, the client can use the message IDs in the reference field to group all messages in the thread together.

Mail clients and servers

E-mail is managed with an e-mail client, which may be an application installed locally on the computer, or it may be web-based, in which case it is accessed through a web browser. Some advantages of an installed mail application are the ability to copy messages to a local store, and to access them offline, which is useful when there is a need to analyze a large quantity of messages and somewhat more sophisticated user interfaces. The main advantage of web-based clients is that your mail can be accessed from any computer with a web browser. Web-based email comes in two forms. Your organization's mail server may provide a web page which accesses mail on its servers. The other alternative is an independent mail provider such as Yahoo!, Google or MSN. The mail on these sites will be completely separate from your organization.

In a web-based client, the storage and access of mail is handled entirely by the remote mail server and is completely hidden from the user. Locally installed mail client applications need to be able to access a mail box or mail store. If the local computer is a mail server, then the mail store may be on the local file system, but, much more likely, the mail client is used to access a mail store on separate mail server. The mail client needs to be set up with the correct connection parameters to the mail server. There are a few different protocols for communication between mail clients and mail servers, among them POP and IMAP, which are internet standards, and MAPI, which is a Microsoft protocol. The choice of mail applications depends to some extent on what computer platform you are using

(Windows, Mac, etc....), and what mail server software is being used by your mail provider, which might be your employer; beyond that there is some room for user preference. We will summarize some of the more common mail applications. A much more detailed summary can be viewed at Wikipedia (http://en. wikipedia.org/wiki/Comparison_of_e-mail_clients, http://en.wikipedia.org/ wiki/Comparison_of_webmail_providers).

If your organization's computer systems are largely Windows based, then the mail server is likely to be **Microsoft Exchange**; and if your computer runs Windows, then the choice of mail client will probably be Microsoft Office **Outlook** (sometimes just known as Outlook). This is very common in businesses and somewhat less common in college settings. Outlook is well integrated with Exchange, and, beyond providing mail capability using POP, IMAP or MAPI (in later versions of Outlook), also allows calendaring, task lists, and contact lists on the server. Newer versions also provide an RSS feed reader (RSS is discussed in a later chapter). Outlook is part of the Microsoft Office suite. Other mail clients are perfectly capable of accessing an Exchange server mail store using either POP or IMAP, but likely will not have the same calendar and contact tools. Similarly, Outlook can access mail from another type of mail server, but will be limited to mail over POP or IMAP.

Microsoft Outlook Express, also on Windows, is a product distinct from Office Outlook, despite the similar name. It can get mail via POP and IMAP, but not with MAPI. Recent versions of Outlook Express are integrated with Windows Messenger IM client. Starting with Windows Vista, Microsoft is replacing Outlook Express with a product called **Windows Live Mail**.

Mozilla Thunderbird and **Mozilla SeaMonkey** are the descendants of the **Netscape Communicator** web and mail application suite. SeaMonkey is a complete suite and includes browser, mail client, news and RSS reader. Thunderbird is a smaller application and just includes the mail, news and RSS clients. They communicate with a mail server with POP or IMAP. These applications are available in very nearly the same form on Windows, Mac OS X and on Linux. Thunderbird and SeaMonkey are available for free via download (http://www.mozilla.org).

The Mac OS X operating environment comes with the **Apple Mail** application included. Apple Mail can access e-mail using POP or IMAP. Beyond e-mail it integrates with other Apple applications such as **Address Book, iChat** and **iCal**.

Microsoft Office for Mac OS X, includes a mail application called **Entourage**, which is intended to be similar in function to Outlook on Windows. It also includes some calendar, address book and organization functions. It has some integration with Microsoft Exchange, but not quite to the level of Outlook on the Windows platform.

In Linux there are many choices; among them **Evolution** and **Kmail** as well as the **Mozilla** applications. **Evolution** has e-mail, address book and calendar functions.and is designed to be similar to Microsoft Office

Outlook. **Kmail** is one of many applications that are part of the **KDE** desktop environment, and in combination with them provides email, calendaring and instant messaging. There are also some purely command line mail clients such as **pine** and **mutt**. There are occasions when a non-graphical environment is required, but usually it is much preferable to use one of the graphically oriented applications.

If you are not associated with an organization with the ability to provide mail service, or even if you want to keep mail distinct from mail at your place of employment, you can use web-based mail facilities such as **MSN Hotmail**, **Yahoo! Mail**, or **Google Gmail**, and others. These services are ad-supported and free, with perhaps additional premium services. They typically provide several gigabytes of mail storage, which is adequate for most users.

MSN Hotmail is currently being renamed as **Windows Live Hotmail**. Your sign-in is called your Windows Live ID, and could be a Microsoft Passport, MSN Hotmail or MSN Messenger account. This sign-in is valid for all those services, as well as others such as Zune and Xbox Live. Currently 5 GB of mail storage are available, but these limits change with time.

Yahoo! Mail is currently the free mail service with the largest user base. There is no limit on mail storage, but individual messages including attachments may be no larger than 10 MB. A Yahoo! account also provides access to **Yahoo! Messenger** chat client, **Yahoo! Groups** for email groups and the **Flickr** photo site.

Google Mail (or Gmail) is a more recent entry into the free web-based email environment. It initially offered 1 GB of mail storage, which at the time was more than the others, and forced them to expand their capacity; now it offers about 3 GB for free and more for a charge. A Google log-in provides access to a large number of Google online applications, such **Google Documents**, **Google Calendar**, and the **Picasa** picture service. Google seems like it is aiming to eventually be a complete alternative to in-house applications.

As far as your research goes, there is little reason to be concerned about which email application you use. All the mail clients and services listed above have the functions necessary communicate surveys and interviews. The choice will be mostly determined by other factors, such as your preferences for certain features and institutional or ISP (Internet Service Provider) requirements. Most of the mail clients listed are able to display embedded formatting and graphics in the message display. Some clients may have features that make them useful. For example, the message inbox view in Apple Mail will highlight all messages in a thread in color when one of them is selected. Google Mail groups messages by subject by default.

Occasional difficulties in communicating with a participant may occur due to other technical issues, however. For example, institutions or services may block incoming messages from a particular address. There can be any number of reasons for such a block, the most common being to do with spam relays (unsolicited email messages often sent in bulk) coming from a particular internet address. To stop a relay, a system administrator could block all messages from a given domain for a particular period of time. The key point, however, is that the problem is not a reflection of email incompatibility, but rather a reflection of a domain issue.

Group addressing and listservers

When email is used to communicate with a moderate to large number of people, as might be the case with a focus group, managing the address list can lead to several problems. At a minimum, if there are multiple exchanges to the same group of recipients, then the group should be in an email client address book. Most every mail client has some function for maintaining address books. However, if there is a need to share a group address, this becomes more difficult. In particular, if recipients need to be added and or subtracted more than occasionally, then keeping the group address synchronized becomes onerous. The solution to this is to create a group on a listserver.

Listservers (sometimes called listservs) are applications that run on a mail service provider server, and are used to maintain a possibly dynamic list of recipients. Participants on the listserver address mail to the listserver address, and the listserver software handles the distribution to the actual recipients. A listserver list has a designated owner, and there are usually several options for the list owner to control who may read the list and post to the list. Typically a user must submit a request to join or access the list; which at minimum means that the listserver forwards messages addressed to the list to the user. It usually means that the user may also send messages to the list; but this need not be so. Frequently there are also controls that enable the list owner to allow only select members to post to the list and limit everyone to reading; or else allow the owner to moderate, or selectively approve, any submissions to the list. Some listservers also have options to make the list message archive available for search or download.

Some of the many listserver products are Mailman (open source, Linux/Unix, OSX, Windows) (http://www.gnu.org/software/mailman/), LISTSERV (commercial, Windows, Unix) (http://www.lsoft.com/products/listserv.asp), Majordomo (open source Linux/Unix) (http://www.greatcircle.com/majordomo/), and MailList King (commercial, Windows) (http://www.xequte.com/maillistking/). Another option is to use a hosted service such as the free (ad-based) Yahoo! Groups (http://groups.yahoo.com), or MSN Groups (http://groups.msn.com/home), or a commercial hosted service like SimpleList (http://www.simplelists.com/). Yahoo! Groups and MSN Groups have a limitation that all members of one of their groups must have Yahoo! Mail or MSN Live Mail mail accounts, respectively. This may preclude these group mail servers from many situations.

Things to consider before deciding on an option are ease of access, archiving needs, whether or not digesting is a necessary feature, and whether or not there is a means for hosting a service independent from an online service. The easiest, and arguably most popular, method is to host a listserver. Your enter-prise may have some listserver software installed on the mail server. If you will be installing and managing your own listserver, **Mailman** is open source and free, and is easy to set up. Listservers can be moderated, enabling a researcher to closely manage membership and participation such as in a focus group, or unmoderated, where a researcher may want to lurk to see who joins and par-ticipates, or to participate in a topical discussion. An unmoderated list that is closed enables participants to join on their own, but requires the list owner to approve all subscriptions to the list.

Many listservers can be managed by sending specially crafted emails to an administrative address on the server. Users can request to be added to an existing list by sending a message to the listserver. Often this message takes the form of 'SUBSCRIBE listname your name' as in Majordomo or Listserver. The list-server will then usually reply with a message requesting the recipient to con-firm their subscription. This is done to foil (to some extent) spam email address harvesters. Mailman is managed entirely through a web site and Listserver also has a web management interface available. Potential recipients can request to be added by visiting the web site. The management interface is very intuitive. Each product will have commands for the list owner to add users explicitly (instead of letting them add themselves), or change the moderation level or other policies. The exact format will depend on the product. Documentation can be found at the product web site.

Mail stores

In some types of analysis, the researcher will want to scan large numbers of messages. Doing this through the mail client interface will usually be very inconvenient. It may be better to scan the mail storage files directly. Mail servers store mail messages in a variety of formats. Some are text files while others are in a proprietary database format. Mail boxes on servers are gen-erally not directly available to users; the system administrator would need to give explicit permission to access it. However, for your own mail account, mail clients who connect to a server with the POP or IMAP generally save a copy of each message on the client machine. They also usually offer an option of creating a local mail box so you can use that function to separate out mail messages. If you want to convert the mail box into a text file for analysis, the method depends on the mail client. Unix/Linux clients often store local mail boxes in "mbox" format. The format is basically the raw message format with two additional lines of text. Each message starts with a "From" line (note that there is no":") and is followed by the raw mail con-tents, which are then followed by a blank line. The next message follows the blank line and is marked by the next "From" line.

From gaiser@springer.net
Return-Path: <gaiser@springer.net>
Received: from [] (account gaiser@springer.net [136.255.255.167] verified)
  by fe2.isp.net(CommuniGate Pro SMTP 5.0.13)
  with ESMTPSA id 231521637 for gaiser@springer.net; Fri, 28 Sep 2007
  15:38:02 -0400
Mime-Version: 1.0 (Apple Message framework v752.3)
Content-Transfer-Encoding: 7bit
Message-Id: <A16E0CA3-57FC-4157-B85F-AC460D2CA39B@surfsup.
com>
Content-Type: text/plain; charset=US-ASCII; format=flowed
To: Schreiner Tony <schreiner@surfsup.net>
From: Ted Gaiser <gaiser@springer.net>
Subject: manuscript
Date: Fri, 28 Sep 2007 15:38:13 -0400
X-Mailer: Apple Mail (2.752.3)
Hi Tony
Have you done the changes for chapter 3 yet?
Ted

From afriend@yahoo.com
...

Thunderbird also uses the mbox format. On OS X, the files are stored under the user's home directory in Library/Thunderbird/Profiles/default/xxxxxxxx. slt/ImapMail (or just Mail for local folders). On Windows XP,the files are stored in the subdirectory AppData\Thunderbird\Profiles\xxxxxxxx.default\ Mail; on Windows Vista the files are stored in the subdirectory AppData\ Roaming\Thunderbird\Profiles\Mail, under the user's home directory. Note that AppData is a hidden folder by default and the user needs to go to the Folder Options control panel to make it visible.

Another possible format, which is used by the Apple Mail application, is to store each message in a separate file. They are stored under the user's home directory in Library/Mail subdirectory. The files typically have names which identify their message ID to the mail client, but are not very useful to the user. But they are text files which can be read by a user or application.

Microsoft mail clients like Outlook store their mail boxes in the PST (Personal Information Store) format. This is a binary format and not easy to access directly. The mail client would have to be used to save each message as text. The new Windows Mail in Vista does, however, save mail files as text files.

Having considered the public-face and behind-the-scenes aspects of email, now let us look at how email might be used for social research.

Using email for surveys

Many people use email to distribute surveys either in the body of an email message or as an attachment. While this is fine, it has limited advantages over sending a survey through the post or asking people to complete a survey in a particular location. Essentially, it provides easier access to a wide audience and saves on postage. There are, however, a few pitfalls to consider when sending surveys in email and expecting completed surveys in a reply. Survey documents are often formatted in a certain way to enhance the categories of questions or the choice of answers. Since mail message are plain text and do not always preserve formatting because of line folding, it becomes tempting to send the survey as an attached word processing document or PDF file. But this relies on the recipient having the software necessary to modify these documents as they respond to the question, and then they have to attach it to a reply email. This is generally more work than should be expected of a survey target. If the survey is sent as plain text in the message, the author of the survey needs to take some care that the answer sections are obvious, and that the recipient can easily enter answers into a reply message without drastically altering the appearance of the survey.

Another major benefit lost when emailing a survey rather than creating an online survey and emailing a link is data entry. Emailed equivalents to paper surveys require manual data entry, though some assistance can be provided by text-parsing tools. Most often these tools are custom written scripts in perl and require some programming expertise.

The alternative to emailing the survey and reading the reply is to put a survey up on a web site and use email to send a URL link to the web site and a request for the recipient to visit the web site. The web server and associated programs can then be used to automate the data entry. One note, however: it is considered risky to the user to click on links in email messages because scammers often use this to direct unaware users to web sites that download malware to the user's computer. It is considered safer to copy the web address into the web browser address window using copy and paste operations. Another factor to consider in sending out a survey invitation is whether the wording for such an invitation is similar to that used in spam messages. If the author does not take some care in the wording, the invitation might wind up in many recipients' junk mail folders without them ever seeing it. And another factor that is independent of which technology is used to distribute a survey, is that the level of response to surveys solicited by email is lower than more personal requests, and the respondents will be more self-selected, and therefore bias may be introduced.

Using email for interviews

Email provides an easy and manageable means for conducting interviews. Rather than having to capture the data in real-time such as in a chat session, email provides a readily accessible documentation of a discussion. In addition, while some may consider it advantageous to capture "off-the-cuff" responses to questions, it is possible to access a greater depth of response when the interviewee has the ability to think through a substantive response (Gaiser, 2000). As with any research endeavor, it is important for researchers to remember to seek permission. It may be easy to slide into a discussion via email that simply feels like an in-depth discussion, and that you decide you want to use as data as you move forward with your research. If you're interacting via email for research purposes, or think your discussion may lead to a research exercise, be sure to ask the participant's permission.

When initially outlining your research endeavor, it's also important to establish the scope of your work. What your expectation is, how long you think your interaction will take, how many topics you are likely to cover, and so forth. Given you'll be interacting online, it's extremely helpful to manage a participant's expectations. If, on the other hand, you choose not to do so, you run the risk of losing a participant part way through the interview.

As an aid to "discussion," almost all email clients will include the original message in a reply, and mark it with a leading ">" character or some other symbol. Reply styles can be either top-post, bottom-post or in-line; in which, respectively, the reply goes above the original, below the original, or is interspersed with the original. The style can be a matter of personal preference, but bottom-posting is easier to follow if there are many exchanges such as in an interview, because the exchanges are ordered in the message as they would be in a written document. In-line posting helps when several points need to be addressed; the response can be adjacent to the related point. However, many mail clients top-post by default, and some will not allow any other option (most commonly on compact mobile devices such as a Palm personal assistant). There is no way to force respondents to use any particular style; the only thing that can be done is to ask.

Given the loss of visual cues in online interviewing (and online focus groups), participants and researchers do not have the opportunity to see each other's face, experience body language, and so forth. One of the ways in which a researcher can make the difference between failure and success is by being emotionally present online (Feig, 1989). Verbal cues such as added language inserted into the text: `I don' t know anything about that [ sigh];` using symbols (☺); using upper- and lower-case lettering – I DON'T KNOW anything about that; using formatting to add emphasis – I **don't** know anything about that; and question evasion, all communicate something. A good researcher will be "present" and use skills to identify, address and learn from online verbal cues.

Using email for an interview is quite common. Issues with online interviewing vary with disciplines, but in general all attempt to reach a broad group of participants, expedite and streamline the process of interviewing, save on costs and possibly expedite time to publication. [e.g. White, 2005, (http://www.webpronews.com/ebusiness/contentandcopywriting/wpn-6-20050727EmailInterviews.html).

The following is a case example of an interview for a research study on an online community. Note the way in which the research participant responds to the interviewer's questions, choosing specific sections of the interview and integrating them into the response. The text has been altered from the original mail message. Originally it would have a quote level for each iteration of the message passing back and forth, as well as the user name and time of the response. These mark-ups can distract from the message content so for presentation purposes it is better to format it as follows.

SAMPLE EMAIL INTERVIEW

Hello:

I trust you had a good break. You had indicated I should contact you around the 1st of April. Here I am. Are you ready to get started? I hesitated about starting because I am going away for the weekend. But I figured I could send along the first questions, and if you happen to get to them prior to my departure, then we can go a couple rounds before I leave. If not, you'll probably have a reply for me upon my return.

So here goes. Why don't we begin with you telling me a little about why you join a discussion group? What are your motivating factors? And how do you find online groups? through friends? postings? lists? ...

When you have joined a group(s), do you ever get a sense of "belonging?" Do you ever feel like, "I belong here?" If yes, why? What gives you the feeling? Does something transpire that leaves you feeling like you "belong? If not, what do you think is missing that might enable you to feel like you "belong?"

I look forward to your response.

==

I joined two groups back when there were only three nursing discussion groups. One is for nursing research – its first name was [discussion list] and the other is the nursing informatics list. I have stayed with both of those groups. I honestly do not remember how I heard of [discussion list] – the informatics group. It was the first group I joined that I stayed on. I was part of the [discussion list] group before and I am not a statistician, so did

(Continued)

not belong. I believe that a colleague told me about it. The other group was posted to the [discussion list] list. Now I find groups by doing listserv searches, but mostly the ones that I stay with are word of mouth or should I say word of email.

>When you have joined a group(s), do you ever get a sense of "belong-ing?" Do you ever feel
>like, "I belong here." If yes, why? What gives you the feeling?

Very much so. All three groups that I actively participate with are from practice groups that are in isolation to other health care providers (school nurses) or others with that expertise – there is no one in our workplaces who shares our orientation or our concerns or have our expertise. I depend on these list to keep me updated on the latest trends, buzz words, the latest good publications and support and, yes, friendship. We have had face-to-face meetings with 2 of the groups that I am on at profes-sional conferences. We had 60 people attend a luncheon in San Antonio [discussion list] and the school nurses identify themselves at conferences all over the country by putting green dots on their name tags. This year the NASN offered to pick up the tab for ribbons for our badges (you know the type that usually say speaker, these say XXXXX).

I feel like I know these people better than people I see every day. Our get-togethers are hysterical; you would think it is a group of long lost rela-tives, not a group of people who have never laid eyes on each other. We know each other very well before the conversations even start so there is no warming-up period.

>Does something transpire that leaves you feeling like you "belong?" If not, what do you
>think is missing that might enable you to feel like you "belong?"

You get lots of feedback, both directed to the whole group – isn't what Martha just said so wonderful, or to you personally. If you post about a really trying experience the empathy is palpable. This is especially for the school nurses list. WE have all been there when a principal does not back you up, or a parent refuses to come to school to pick up a very sick kid or, heaven forbid, you make a mistake. The warmth comes through.

Focus groups with email

Focus group data are discussions taking place among two or more participants with or without the input of a leader. Group mail or listservers are an ideal plat-form for this. The listserver software keeps the messages organized by subject or message thread, and additionally archives the discussion for later downloading. The thing to consider in terms of later analysis is whether the focus group will include previous messages in their replies; this is not necessary because all the messages will be in the archive in the right order, but it is hard to prevent users from doing it because it is usually the default mail client behavior. Another behavior that needs to be set is whether replies from a listserver are sent by default back to the listserver address, or to the sender of the message. Some listservers do one by default and some do the other. If the listserver is set up to reply to the sender rather than the listserver, and if that behavior cannot be changed, then participants have to remember to select 'reply to all', rather than 'reply to sender.'

Online focus groups enable a researcher to access easily a large and, potentially, diverse population, and can be relatively inexpensive to run. The method enables a researcher to access a wide variety of data (in) a very brief period of time (Gaiser, 2008: 669). They are easy to coordinate, have limited technical requirements, the data are easily captured, and there is little to no technical training and skill required for participants to contribute.

It's important to keep in mind, however, that online focus groups also present a variety of challenges. They can be difficult to manage for a moderator, or focus group facilitator. Participants may not feel the same kind of obligation to the moderator that they may in a face-to-face environment, leading them to feel free to do as they please within the group. This concern is heightened in an asynchronous group where participants may be contributing to the discussion when the moderator isn't "present." In this environment, there is a potential loss of the impulse response. "Freudian slips" often reveal a great deal of data for a researcher. Given time to think through a posting before submitting it can have a mediating effect on impulse responses (Gaiser, 2008: 687). The depth of responses, however, should provide a suitable trade-off.

Roles are another odd aspect when conducting focus groups as well as online interviews. As noted elsewhere in the book, interactions mediated through technologies continue to challenge contemporary notions of personal roles. Online, the relationship and roles of participant and moderator continue to evolve. In addition, online participant/observer research in which the researcher sees her or himself as a participant shifts the notion of roles. While role shifting can have its own rewards for particular types of research endeavors, the researcher is encouraged to think through relinquishing the role of facilitator or moderator very carefully. While a group may become self-functioning and provide tremendously rich data, you run the risk of losing participants who feel uncomfortable with no one being charge. This is likely to vary with any number of demographics such as age, education and online experience, but the end result may be the failure of a focus group if some perceive the researcher as stepping away, becoming a participant, or simply not exerting some form of control over the discussion.

When starting a focus group, it's a good idea to use an introductory exercise. It provides the opportunity to engage everyone equally, can set the tone for the group, begins to establish trust, can have the benefit of setting participants at ease and, most importantly, can get the participants to begin functioning as a group.

The following is a sample focus group discussion using a listserv. Notice the extraneous symbols, particularly when a participant replies and includes the previous message. The discussion also takes on a form of its own, with responses directly, indirectly, or not at all responding to previous comments and questions. The tilde (~) represents a break between messages. A "digest" or collection of emails from a listserv discussion does not include a tilde. The tilde was added here for the reader's convenience. It may be useful to note that sometimes a tilde is used to differentiate between participants in a study when inserting text into an analytical application.

SAMPLE FOCUS GROUP DISCUSSION

When another academic and I started [our channel] in October 1993, our aim was to find a compatible, [discussion list], university-based community to operate within, or we would get out of IRC altogether. We had become very close to a small group (8) of like minded people in [another channel] over the months, and had the core of a new channel in mind when [our channel] was created. The ground rules of the new channel were absolutely simple: no racism, no anti Semitism, no sexism, no adolescent nonsense.

Nothing else was explicitly stated, but there was every hope that any new people who came on board would be interested in the same sorts of things as the 10 of us: socialism, religion and society, the peace movement, environmentalism, literature/music/art, family relationships and child rearing, democracy and citizenship etc. etc. And for the first year or so, the hope was fulfilled. Even when people had major differences in attitudes to a particular issue, we had enough of a shared world view to take the differences in our stride. For example, a commitment to "free university education for all citizens" was given a higher priority than "staff–student dating policies".

But as time went on, the original group commitments were overwhelmed by new people coming in, new people who did not know of the original hopes for the group and would not have shared them in any case. Now instead of 50 people, about whom I care greatly, there are 350 people, most of whom I care not one whit about. People are still polite, still not accepting of anti Semitism and racism; but they are younger, more trivial, more right wing, less thoughtful, less academically rigorous.

I still go to the channel each day, to keep in touch as it were. But if there were important issues to discuss, they would now be taken to a limited email group rather than to an open on-line discussion.

Regretfully

H.

~

"Have you ever made a comment that you thought was perfectly acceptable only to discover the group felt otherwise? Elaborate on that/those experience/s. How did it/they feel? Why? What part of that/those experience/s has stayed with you and affected your on-line interactions?"

I have lived in Europe for many years, and thought I understood different societies. Yet I still go into shock when my letters are flamed. This happens mainly when we run into cultural boundaries that, despite my regular trips to America and my very regular virtual contact with Americans, still blow me away. In response to a letter, I will make a perfectly sensible comment that in England, New Zealand, South Africa, Australia or India would not even raise an eyebrow. Yet I am faced with incredulity, at best! For example, I could not conceive of any citizen being allowed to have a gun in his house, and would expect anyone with a gun to be imprisoned. As far as I know, any sensible Commonwealth citizen would think that ... it is not a radical thought in the slightest. Yet I have seen some American [discussion list members] dismiss my views out of hand, thinking I am either a dreamer or a left wing ratbag or worse.

The trouble is, whereas one knows perfectly well not to taunt Arabs about Hebron, there is no way of knowing in advance what otherwise perfectly mainstream view in Commonwealth countries will receive this hostile and demeaning reaction from some Americans. Universal health care? Mandatory voting for all citizens? Migration laws? Pensions for the unemployed? Unionization of work sites?

My response is to be honest and open only during the hours when the western hemisphere is asleep (my apologies to Canadians) and at other times, to be very cautious about expressing philosophical views. On one hand, the _joy_ of irc is to spread one's exposure to people we would not normally meet in our own society. On the other hand, the _misery_ of irc is when those very same people are totally dismissive of one's belief system.

~

> mind when [our channel] was created. The ground rules of the new channel were absolutely simple: no
> racism, no anti-semitism, no sexism, no adolescent nonsense.

(Continued)

>
> Nothing else was explicitly stated, but there was every hope that any new people who came on
> board would be interested in the same sorts of things as the 10 of us: socialism, religion and
> society, the peace movement, environmentalism, literature/music/art, family relationships and
> child rearing, democracy and citizenship etc. etc. And for the first year or so, the hope was
> fulfilled. Even when people had major differences in attitudes to a particular issue, we had enough
> of a shared world view to take the differences in our stride. For example, a commitment to "free
> university education for all citizens" was given a higher priority than "staff-student dating policies".
> But as time went on, the original group commitments were overwhelmed by new people coming
> in, new people who did not know of the original hopes for the group and would not have shared
> them in any case. Now instead of 50 people, about whom I care greatly, there are 350 people, most
> of whom I care not one whit about. People are still polite, still not accepting of anti Semitism and
> racism; but they are younger, more trivial, more right wing, less thoughtful, less academically
> rigorous.
> I still go to the channel each day, to keep in touch as it were. But if there were important issues to
> discuss, they would now be taken to a limited email group rather than to an open on-line
> discussion
>
> Regretfully
> H.

~

I also see the private email groups forming out of the larger groups, and for much the same reason. There are simply some things that, for one reason or another, one doesn't want to put out in front of the whole group, whether it be an important issue that one wants to be treated as such, or a private matter.

As the groups grow larger and larger, this back-channel situation occurs more often.

DJ

~

One of the groups I belong to has over 600 members, but most of the posting is done by about 20 individuals. Right now the list is having an identity crisis of sorts, and those who do the posting will be determining the outcome. But this is the way in any group, I think; the ones who participate the most carry the most weight, especially in view of the fact that we have no way of knowing who the lurkers are.

As far as forming a community vs. academic concerns, I DON'T see any difference between the two. A group's major function may be to discuss academically, but the fact that it is a group of people automatically makes it a community.

J.

~

One of the things I seem to be hearing is there is a natural evolutionary process going on with communities much like any community (in RL) that we might belong to. In some groups, the norms have changed. In others, members are moving on to new groups (beginning with extensive back-channel discussions that lead to new groups), hence the old groups sound as if they are splitting up into separate factions.

Are we saying that on-line groups go through the same evolutionary process that any other group we might belong to does? Do "charters" (or maybe FAQs is a better word) get rewritten? Has anyone been a member of a group that changed its understanding of itself? (Forgive me, but my mind has wandered to the Monty Python knights that "used to be the knights that said neat" and "now are the knights that say 'icky'.") But seriously, has anyone experienced this type of group transformation? Or do the information files of a group get revised on-goingly?

Another point I would like people to explore/consider is the idea of participating somewhere on the Net where we feel our understanding of reality is somewhat dismissed by others. Someone used the expression "dismissive of my beliefs." I have continued to participate in groups where my thinking certainly wasn't the norm because I had managed to "get" something from the experience. What is the hook for you that keeps you

(Continued)

going back to places that might not agree with your opinions, cultural perspective, or any number of things (such as if they knew you were gay/lesbian, a woman/man, handicapped/or not, ...)?

T

~

>What do others think about this? Is it possible for "the few" to assert their will on the others? What
>was different about this event as opposed to the harrassing boy scouts that encountered the
>opposition of other list members?

Actually, as I indicated obliquely, a surprising number of people jumped on the few self-appointed 'censors'. Some were supportive of their efforts, but many were not.

>The other comment I would like to hear more on (from anyone) is on "forming a community" vs. a
>group to "discuss academic concerns." What's the difference? Why is there a difference to some >people and maybe not others?

I think a group doesn't become a community until it faces a common problem that threatens the group's existence and they come together to deal with it. For example, the newsgroup xxx.yyyyy.xxx was started about a year ago for pacific islanders and others with an interest there could have a place to meet and 'talk'. It started off well, but soon was innundated by massive, inflammatory cross-posts from unrelated groups, with off-color topics like 'asian women like ...'.

Recently a core group has begun an effort to turn the group into a moderated group, with the principal goal to filter out the off-topic and unrelated cross-posts. (I couldn't read the group if my reader didn't have kill filters. My kill file still cuts out over 50% of the total traffic, but it was as high as 80%.) We are trying really hard to bring this off and although it means significant shared hard work, we think we will do it.

So, I think some underlying bond or challenge or reason to be together needs to be there.

B.

~

>Are we saying that on-line groups go through the same evolutionary process that any other group >we might belong to does?

Yes, I would say it is very similar, only the means of communication is different.

>Do "charters" (or maybe FAQs is a better word) get rewritten? Has any-one been a member of a >group that changed its understanding of itself?

FAQs change regularly in most groups. 'Charter' (at least in the usenet newsgroup sense) does not, without a formal voting process, as there is a sort of over-riding admin structure (if people are willing to follow it) for the 'big-8' groups (rec. comp. soc. news. etc).

>Have you been part of groups that changed?

Yes. A good example is the rec.scouting newsgroup. This used to be a good place for Scouting people to exchange ideas. Then it got invaded by some religious bigots who were opposed to the Boy Scouts of America's policy of not allowing gays to be Scout Leaders or another policy that requires a boy to have some kind of a religious belief (it specifically doesn't say what kind, but suggests there should be some belief).

Huge vitriolic flame-wars resulted, cross-posted to various religious groups. Posts grew from 30 lines, to 300, to 3000 lines. People were call-ing each other names, YELLING and ****screaming****!!!!! etc.

I quit reading it for about 6 months and then started to creep back into it. There weren't very many people left in the resulting wasteland. The orig-inal idea of exchange had been subverted. However, a group of people undertook a revision of the newgroup, and in fact proposed 5 new groups to replace the old one (USA, International, Politics, Girl Scouts, Misc). The charters for each were hammered out in open discussion, alterations were made and re-argued and eventually voted on. Now, the group is larger than before and discussions are civil, and open exchanges.

B.

~

Just so I'm clear, B., do you mean "by consensus" when you say that the new group arrangements were "hammered out in open discussion?", or do you mean a few people (or one person) listened to the group's thoughts and then said "this is what we're going to do?" (And thanks for sharing that experience.)

T

~

>Just so I'm clear, B., do you mean "by consensus" when you say that the new group arrangements

(Continued)

>were "hammered out in open discussion?", or do you mean a few people (or one person) listened
>to the group's thoughts and then said "this is what we're going to do?" (And thanks for sharing
>that experience.)

Well, there was a core of 6-8 people who drafted the formal 'Request for Discussion' msgs, and kind of coordinated the discussion, but something over 175 people commented on various parts of the proposals, and we went through 5 drafts to get the 6th and final one that was actually voted on. The core group mostly was silent and let others make comments, suggestions, etc., responding with revised wordings, asking questions only to clarify points, etc. This was how we discovered we needed to make a separate group for girl scouts.

So I'd say it was very much a large group consensus building activity, not a small clique just saying 'here's what we'll do'.

B.

~

> One of the things I seem to be hearing is there is a natural evolutionary process going on with
> communities much like any community (in RL) that we might belong to. In some groups, the
> norms have changed. In others, members are moving on to new groups (beginning with extensive
> back- channel discussions that lead to new groups), hence the old groups sound as if they are
> splitting up into separate factions.

I have seen it happen both ways. A few will break off from the original group in order to facilitate what they perceive to be "their" purpose. You know, sometimes I think the problem simply lies with semantics. Parts of a group aren't coming from the same frame of reference as other parts of the group; thus, even though they are basically saying the same thing, they aren't understanding each other.

> Are we saying that on-line groups go through the same evolutionary process that any other group > we might belong to does? Do "charters" (or maybe FAQs is a better word) get rewritten? Has
> anyone been a member of a group that changed its understanding of itself? (Forgive me, but my
> mind has wandered to the Monty Python knights that "used to be the knights that said neat" and

> "now are the knights that say 'icky'.") But seriously, has anyone experienced this type of group
> transformation? Or do the information files of a group get revised ongoingly?

Sure they do. Nothing stays the same (even though some might wish it); if it stays absolutely the same, what do you have? Stasis. And you know what stasis equals.

I have also seen groups, formed around a central belief, but not necessarily a purpose, make itself up as it goes along.

Oh, and yes, FAQs change too. Sometimes it's just for the purpose of updating personnel; other times it's because the group's purpose has changed or new rules have been deemed necessary.

> Another point I would people to explore/consider is the idea of participating somewhere on the
> Net where we feel our understanding of reality is somewhat dismissed by others. Someone used
> the expression "dismissive of my beliefs." I have continued to participate in groups where my
> thinking certainly wasn't the norm because I had managed to "get" something from the experience.
> What is the hook for you that keeps you going back to places that might not agree with your
> opinions, cultural perspective, or any number of things (such as if they knew you were gay/lesbian,
> a woman/man, handicapped/or not, ...)?
>
> T

The reason I continue to frequent certain groups that differ from either my take on life, or my belief system, whatever, is that I am interested in learning what other people think and why. I am fascinated by all types of cultural experiences; culture in general. I WANT to hear what people unlike me are thinking and what they believe.

After all, ya never know when ya might just learn somethin'!

DJ

This rather long example is provided as an illustration of what to expect in a focus group discussion. There are a number of items illustrating early points worth noting. For example, some of the discussion flows rather well with questions being followed directly with answers. In other cases, the discussion appears somewhat disjointed and disconnected, with responses being unrelated to a particular question, or answers being given to questions that were asked several posts prior. In some cases, responses are to questions posed by other participants and not directly related to the questions asked. The use of the ">" symbol also provides a way for a participant to insert questions as a way of indicating which question is being addressed.

In the text, the use of symbols, and of specific punctuation, and of text is actually discussed. One participant notes that sometimes people are "YELLING and ****screaming****!!!!!." One participant noted, "I WANT to hear what people unlike me are thinking," using "WANT" to highlight his point. In another example, the participant emphasizes his point by stating, "I DON'T see any difference between the two" with "DON'T" adding emphasis. In each case, the added emphasis may aid the researcher in picking up on a particular sentiment or underlying issue worth further exploration.

Another issue illustrated in the example is the issue of jargon. Often in online discussions, people will assume a familiarity with jargon. Terms like F2F, which means face-to-face, FAQ, frequently asked questions, and RL, real life, will appear in a response. Researchers need to be prepared to decipher online jargon to ensure that they understand the meaning of a participant's contribution.

In the preceding pages we've outlined the ways in which email functions and how it can be used in research for interviews, surveys and focus. A number of issues related to working the environment and using these research techniques have been identified to aid a researcher. There are case examples and practical tips for getting started. As you move beyond the beginning stages and seek more sophisticated information to support your efforts, we encourage you to consult the online help for a given software application as well as the tutorials contained within most applications, as well as seek the advice contained in specific methods texts, as outlined in the previous chapters.

5 RESEARCHING USING INSTANT MESSAGING AND CHAT

Chapter summary

- Instant Messaging is synchronous communication
- Internet Relay Chat
- Using IRC
- Running a chat room

The previous chapter covered email, which is an asynchronous form of communication, in which there is not necessarily a relationship between the order that two correspondents read and write messages because of possible delays in the transmission of the messages. Instant Messaging and Chat technologies are considered synchronous: the message appears directly on the recipient's computer regardless of whether the recipient is composing a message or not. Synchronous online communication has become more popular and is growing, especially with younger users; it is safe to anticipate that in the not-to-distant future it will be normative. As such, it is becoming a viable option for researchers to conduct interviews and focus groups.

When considering IM for research, there are the typical challenges of discerning the most appropriate and user-friendly software, as well as making sure everyone has access to a client and the administrative privilege to install it on their computer. When employed, however, the advantages can be formidable. Data are collected more rapidly than in an email method, the interaction has a feel more like that of a traditional interview or focus group, and log files are often cleaner due to fewer identifiers and less extraneous information than appear in an email digest. In the following pages, we will offer information about Instant Messaging and Chat, and provide some advice for how to establish a chat channel for conducting research.

Instant messaging

Instant messaging (IM) is, as the name implies, communication that goes directly from the sender to one or more recipient computers. IM messages are not stored on a server, but may be logged on the sending or receiving system; so the recipient has to be currently online to receive a message (with some exceptions). This provides some advantage in that the sender can usually tell if the addressee is online and able to read the message right away. However, some IM systems do allow offline messages to recipients not currently logged in, so there is some blurring of the distinction between IM and email.

Instant messaging can certainly be used to conduct one-on-one interviews and the experience would be similar to an interview conducted on the telephone, although intonations would be lost. The advantage is that the interview would be immediately transcribed on to the messaging window, noting who the speaker is and also, optionally, the time. For most IM clients, the text of the message needs to be copied and pasted from the window into a document to save it; but many have preferences or settings that allow for the logging or archiving of any exchanges made while the client is connected.

Instant messaging originated on the early multi-user timesharing computer systems of the 1960s, and allowed conversational communication between users logged on the computer. When computer networking became common in the 1980s, these facilities were extended to allow messaging between different computers. Bulletin Board Systems (BBS) became popular during this time as a platform where users could log in specifically for online communication with other users. Many BBSs started with telephone modem connections, but eventually became Internet connected sites.

America Online (AOL) was one of the early large online portals that provided various forms of information but, importantly for the present chapter, included a graphical user interface (GUI) to an instant messaging system it called **AIM**. Another popular early GUI-based IM system was **ICQ**, which was eventually purchased by AOL and folded into AIM. Soon, Microsoft got into the game with **MSN Messenger** (now known as **Windows Live**), and also Yahoo! with **Yahoo! Messenger**. Unfortunately though, unlike modern email, most IM systems are not compatible with other IM systems; each uses its own protocol. AIM uses protocols called OSCAR or TOC, MSN uses MSNP, Yahoo! uses YMSG, and there is a newer protocol called XMPP, which is an open protocol that, it is hoped, will be used by several clients. Mostly these do not inter-operate, so that in general there can be no messages between different systems and users wishing to use multiple systems must use multiple messaging clients. However, there are some clients that can understand more than one protocol. A fairly complete matrix of compatibilities can be found at http://en.wikipedia.org/wiki/Comparison_of_instant_messaging_clients. We'll summarize a few of them.

AOL Instant Messenger (AIM) is free to use (ad-supported) and has clients for Windows and Mac OS. The protocol is proprietary but there are server non-AOL clients that can inter-operate with it. As one of the earliest IM platforms, AIM has a very large user base.

Windows Live Messenger is for Windows platforms only. The protocol is proprietary but can inter-operate with Yahoo! Messenger users. It allows offline messaging and file sharing.

Yahoo! Messenger is free to use and has clients for Windows and Mac OS. One can also send and receive messages from the Yahoo! Mail web site, but the reponse rate is much slower than with the Messenger client. The protocol is proprietary, but users can inter-operate with the Windows Live Messenger network. It allows voice and file sharing.

Google Talk is free to use with a Google account. There is only a Windows client at this time. It uses the open XMPP protocol. Logs are saved automatically. It allows voice and file sharing. Google also has a web-based Chat client that connects to IRC sites.

Apple iChat is for Mac OSX (version 10.4 and higher). It supports the fee-based .Mac network as well as AIM and XMPP. It allows voice and video.

Pidgin is an open-source application that can be installed on Linux or Windows. It supports a wide variety of protocols, including AIM, IRC, MSN, XMPP, Yahoo! and others.

Adium is a client for Mac OSX, and uses the same code library as pidgin, so has many of the same network capabilities.

Jabber/XMPP is a protocol rather than a client. But its open nature means that XMPP servers can be installed at any site, to build a private instant messaging network with all the capabilities that XMPP provides. This may be useful in some circumstances.

Chat

Chat is a generalization of instant messaging where the communication is with a group rather than one-on-one. The protocols are often the same, and many of the IM services and their client applications also support chat facilities.

Internet Relay Chat (IRC)

The best known chat protocol is IRC. Though outwardly similar to instant messaging, interaction with IRC is via an IRC server which uses internet standard protocols. Chat users communicate through a chat client, of which **mIRC** (http://www.mirc.com/) is one of the most common, but available only on Windows.

For Windows, Mac OSX and Linux, there is **Xchat** (http://www.xchat.org/). Pidgin (http://www.pidgin.im/) for Linux and Windows supports many protocols including IRC, as does Adium (http://www.adiumx.com/) for Mac OSX. And for all platforms, the Mozilla browser suite has an extension called **Chatzilla** (http://www.mozilla.org/projects/rt-messaging/chatzilla/) which supports IRC.

Using IRC

Connecting to a chat room is straightforward. We'll show the basics of using IRC (a good tutorial may be found at http://www.irchelp.org/irchelp/irctutorial. html). An IRC client is required. IRC clients operate in two modes. What you type into the input window will be sent to the chat channel and seen by other users. But you can also type in commands, which alter behavior and are not seen by others. IRC commands always begin with the '/' symbol. Most graphical IRC clients have menu pull-down options for the most common commands, so it is typically not necessary to remember them, but it should always be possible to use the command mode directly.

Example:
Connecting to an IRC Channel

You start by setting up a **username** or nickname for yourself; either with a log-in screen for the client, or with the

> /NICK nickname

command. You have to know the IRC channel name you want to interact with and the server that it is hosted on. You can use the menu pull-downs to connect, or type

> /SERVER server-name

> /JOIN #channel-name

and then you will be chatting on the channel, until you use the /LEAVE command. Messages you send to the channel will appear in the discussion window preceded by your nickname, so that everyone can identify the sender. It is also possible to send a message to a single inidividual on the channel, using

> /MSG nickname message

If the channel does not exist when you join it, it is created new and you become the operator. Being the operator allows you to set some policies regarding whether the channel is private or public, whether it is moderated, and whether an invitation to join is required. However, you are only the operator while you remain on the channel. Some networks allow channel registration so that you can keep control of the channel, but not all do.

Running a chat room

Online chat rooms are convenient for conducting "private" interviews and focus groups. They are also a good environment for observing behavior. Chat rooms can be set up on existing IRC servers, or it is possible to install IRC server software on a private server. The best known IRC server software is IRCd which can be downloaded for free from http://www.ircd-hybrid.org/ and installed on Unix/Linux or Windows.

There are a number of issues that should be considered prior to selecting a chat room for purposes of conducting research. Are participants in work environments when they participate? Will their participation in a work environment impede their participation? Some corporations have firewalls that protect their systems and also restrict certain activities. In addition, participants might be constrained by what they will and will not discuss when using an office computer on a company network. In some cases, to conduct a chat room session participants need to download a particular client. Some companies will not allow the installation of applications other than those approved by the company.

While using a chat room can be quick, inexpensive and effective, it can also raise issues for researchers. One significant issue is whether or not the researcher is prepared to serve as technical support. Some systems seem self-evident and easily managed, but not every participant is going to have the same level of sophistication with technology. Some will have issues with their network connection; others will have issues with installation and set-up; some might have difficulty functioning during a chat session. All of the preceding issues require technical assistance. A researcher may feel comfortable using a technology for research, but may not feel competent enough to serve as technical support. In addition, providing technical support during a chat session can serve as a distraction, preventing a researcher from focusing on data collection. Therefore, participants either need to be comfortable with the technology, the researcher needs to be prepared to lose some focus while assisting a participant with a technical problem, and/or there may need to be a technical assistant standing by to assist participants (see Gaiser, 2008).

When using any messaging protocol for research purposes, keep in mind that the actual chat is not the only data available to you. Away messages, for example, can provide a great deal of data (Jacobs, 1999). User profiles also offer data that can be informative and useful for research purposes. Finally, profiles can also provide helpful information for people in the study (ibid.), supplying a context and information about the research.

Example
Sample Chat Discussion

Most IRC applications are graphical, so there will be separate windows for channel status, a list of logged-in users, the traffic on the channel, and the text field where you enter your comments. A brief sample of the channel traffic is shown. We will join a hypothetical IRC channel called #ourchat, employing username 'schreian'. The channel traffic screen shows administrative events with a leading '*', and actual chat leading with the name of the user entering text.

* Now talking on #yourchat
* Topic for #yourchat is: sample chat site
* Topic for #yourchat set by siteowner at Sat Jul 28 11:57:52 2007

A user named 'named' joins.
* named (n=arg@bhe.res-com.wayinternet.com) has joined #yourchat
And then the user named types a comment, followed by a comment by schreian.
<named> hi, when i went to the web site, I could not find the document area.
<schreian> easiest is to follow the help link on the left side.
<named> thanks schreian.
A currently connected user leaves the channel, as does named.
* snowmoon has quit ()
* named has quit ()
And then I leave with the /leave #yourchat command
* You have left channel #yourchat ("Leaving")

Most IRC applications allow the logging of activity while the user is connected. For example, the X-Chat Aqua application on Mac OSX has a logging setting in the Preferences menu. The logs are typically simple text files in the same format as the chat view in the application.

MUDs

MUDs (Multi-user Dungeons) are related to chat rooms with some additional characteristics. Their name derives from the old 'Dungeons & Dragons' game, which was adapted to Unix computers as a single-user game in the late 1970s. The multi-user dungeons are implemented as network-accessible multi-user environments, where communication is enabled, but also feature an internal geography where participants may move around, and where they may add and drop characteristics, and also take certain actions, like nodding, waving and hugging. There can be a scoring system that rewards certain actions, which count when the MUD is used as a game, and many of the earlier MUDs were game sites. They have also developed as educational and social environments, and are used as common discussion areas, albeit often with assumed characters (Cherny, 1999). Users can connect to MUDs with a Telnet terminal application, but will be limited to a purely text-based interface. There are also MUD clients which are designed to enhance the interface to the site. There have been several social studies of MUD sites, typically focusing on the style of communication between users (e.g. Cherney, 1999; Herring, 1996). The increased computational and network power available now means that MUDs are increasingly making way for more visually oriented virtual reality environments, such as the internet game sites which will be described briefly in a later chapter.

Forums

Forums are not precisely instant communication sites, but can be used in similar ways. Forums are typically accessed with a web browser, and are sites where any kind of discussion and information insemination can take place. Being web-based, they usually require an explicit page refresh by the user, or perhaps on automatic refresh every 30 seconds, so the interaction is not immediate, but can still be satisfactory. Specialized applets written in Java or Adobe Flash can make the experience more immediate as well. Many of the social networks also have chat-like facilities. For instance in **Facebook**, joining a group allows you to post messages on a list, which become immediately visible to other logged-in users in the group. And similarly with many blogs (described later), the response section can serve as a kind of chat area.

As with any research method, there are unique benefits and weaknesses. A synchronous discussion with research participants, while providing a more interactive and natural feeling discussion, also brings a number of technical challenges. There is a need to select an appropriate application and ensure that it has the necessary functions, such as being able to create a private channel and to log the discussion. In addition, both support services for the researcher as well as support for participants need to be factored into research planning. Similarly, there may be installation challenges for participants as well as limitations from their location of participation. Finally, a synchronous discussion needs to be arranged and scheduled, so everyone is available at the same time (which, incidentally, may limit who can participate due to time zones, etc.). So while chat provides good opportunities, it should not be pursued unadvisedly.

6 SURVEY RESEARCH ON THE INTERNET

Chapter summary

- The two primary options for developing an online survey are using a web-enabling application such as PHP with a back-end database, or using an online surveying application service provider.
- There are a number of online survey service providers, but before selecting one it should be evaluated carefully for focus, cost and service specifics.
- As with other technical applications, thinking things through prior to embarking on a study can prevent expensive mistakes.

Nearly anyone who has used the internet knows about online surveys. Many of us have received unsolicited invitations to participate in a variety of polls. Do we have particular political leanings, do we care whether or not our respective government allows same-sex couples to get married, do we have particular religious leanings, have we purchased a television in the last six months, will we purchase a car in the next six months, and so on. Sometimes we are "invited" to go to a particular web site via a link sent to us in an email. Other times we make an online purchase and a pop-up invites us to respond to some questions about our experience. At times, it may feel as though online surveys are ubiquitous.

If you are interested in developing an online survey and don't know where to begin, this chapter is for you. The following pages will include general information about survey research. We'll then offer some insights about the online environment and how it compares to traditional survey research. In the latter sections we attempt to provide you with specifics for how to get started, while trying hard not to weigh you down with jargon, which can be a bit intense when discussing online survey developments.

Survey research

Before talking specifically about online surveys, the following is some general information about survey research. Researchers have long known that one of the strengths of survey research is the ability to describe a large population

(Babbie, 2007). This, of course, implies that sampling strategies are important. To be able to make a statement from findings about a given population with some level of assurance, the larger the sample the better. In addition, the more variables on which you would like to analyze a population, the larger your sample needs to be. For example, let's imagine that you are studying access to healthcare. One of your research questions is to see if there are differences in access to services. You might decide you want to analyze on a socio-economic variable to see how access to healthcare services changes by income level. When you begin to break the population into sub-levels of income, the samples in each category decrease considerably. Let's say you have a sample of 500. When you begin to break it by sub-levels of income, you may end up with only 20 or 30 in your upper and lower categories, depending on how you decide to break down income levels. These small numbers in some of the categories will seriously constrain your analysis. As a rule, the more complex the analysis, the larger the sample size should be.

Another aspect of traditional surveys that facilitates the ability to generalize to a larger population is a standardized questionnaire (Babbie, 2007). Everyone participating in the survey needs to answer the same questions. Questionnaires can be broad. But it's important to be mindful that if it is too broad it presents a limitation for the meaning of an answer. In other words, the broader the question, the less meaningful the answer will be. Questions can also be designed to test an idea or conceived notion of the researcher, based on his or her own analytical work before designing the survey instrument.

A limitation of survey research, however, relates directly to question design. Sometimes what we think is important from our perspective may not be what is actually important to others. Designing an instrument that relates to our perspective runs the risk of missing valuable information and insights about a subject. In addition, "surveys cannot measure social action; they can only collect self-reports of recalled past action or of prospective or hypothetical action" (Babbie, 2007: 277). One of the challenges in survey design is to be clear whether or not the topic is measurable through a survey instrument. It is also important to note that it's possible that, by studying a particular subject, there may be an influential effect on a person's opinion (Babbie, 2007). A person may not have formed an opinion until challenged to think about a particular topic in a particular way through the research instrument. These are among several reasons why some researchers prefer qualitative research to survey methods.

Typically, when researchers speak of the ability of their questionnaire to measure a particular social phenomenon, what they are referencing is the concept of *validity*. When speaking of a high level of validity, researchers are making the statement that their questionnaire measures what it was meant to measure. In other words, the findings from a questionnaire can be considered to be a true reflection of a particular phenomenon or issue being studied. Similarly, researchers often speak of *reliability*. What they mean is that a research instrument is reliable if it will provide the same results each time it is administered to the same population. Since we are not attempting to aid you in the actual development and design of your research instrument, beyond this brief discussion, we encourage you to seek other resources on survey design when you begin to develop your instrument.

Web-based surveys

Web technologies make it possible to publish surveys with a potentially very large target audience. Other advantages of web-based surveys are reduced time and costs for data collection, reduction in transcription errors, and the possibility of more sophisticated interactions. As a way of better understanding the specifics of online surveys, you might want to keep in mind the preceding information as you read the following pages. One of the major benefits of going online to conduct your survey research is access to a very broad population. Given the need for large samples, researchers often look to the internet with its possibility of access to a very large population. Be warned, however, that this promise of accessing a large population can be illusive. Many researchers find that response rates can be lower than expected (Witmer, Colman & Katzman, 1999), even though the ease of taking the survey may lead to an expectation of higher return rates. Some suspect that question and instrument length may contribute to low return rates, mindful that attention spans online have a tendency to be short due to the nature of the environment. Witmer et al. (1999) found that there was no significant difference in return rates based on length, suggesting that there may be other issues of concern such as ease of answering questions, interest in the topic, and online interaction with the researcher.

There are some general rules of thumb that researchers can follow to improve response rates. In general, the easier it is to complete a survey, the more likely people will do so. Witmer et al. note that response rates can be improved by avoiding fragmented and varied questionnaires (ibid.: 156). It is also useful to contact potential participants with some type of pre-notification message, explaining the nature of the research, a little about the researchers, any technical details regarding security, how the data will be used, and so forth (Krishnamurthy, 2004). This initial notification could be outlined in such a way as to constitute an informed consent, with the participants' reply of a willingness to participate in the survey as an implied agreement (though researchers are still encouraged to consider including an explanation and formal informed consent as part of the survey instrument).

Tips 'n Tricks

Survey research general advice

- Make research topics interesting and engaging.
- Provide some type of incentive (e.g. a gift certificate, an iPod, or a memory stick).
- Keep survey instruments short. Consider designing several smaller instruments and inviting participants to continue to another section based on their answers to the first section.
- Keep questions short and easy to answer.
- Format responses in a way that makes it easy for participants to complete the survey using check-boxes ☐, radio buttons ○, and text boxes ⬚.
- Send a pre-notification email about your study to potential participants.
- Communicate with participants by sending follow-up notices, potential information about current findings, and a thank-you for participating after they complete the survey.

You'll note we didn't say the population would be large and *diverse*. While some populations have the financial ability and technical skill to access internet resources and others do not, users on the internet change daily. Certainly, everyone, everywhere on the planet, does not have internet access. However, the diversity of the internet is changing rapidly, diminishing the concern about a digital divide among many researchers.

Witmer et al. (1999) found in their research that standard survey methods do not necessarily translate to the computer environment. Participants need incentives to engage them, and persuade them to participate. Many people offer prizes to be given to someone from within a pool of research participants. In most cases, it's fair to assume that the better the incentive, the better the completion rate of your survey. An Apple iPod, for example, is more likely to engage participants than a music CD. In addition, it's important to recruit and contact potential participants in a separate email message. In this way, participants are less likely to feel as though your request is trivial and reflective of the techniques of online marketers seeking their opinion.

Not only do you need to be concerned with the ways in which survey instruments are slightly different in the online environment, but you also need to consider how you will distribute your instrument and collect your data. Some researchers choose to email a survey instrument either in the body of an email message or as an attachment. Others develop a web-based survey. Sometimes they are stand-alone instruments on a website where the hope is that people looking at the site will consider taking the survey. A link to a web-based survey can also be included in the body of a message and emailed to a group of potential participants.

Emailed surveys tend to look and feel like any other instrument you might receive in the mail or be handed by a researcher. It takes no programming skill to paste a survey into the body of an email or attach a word processing document to an email. However, doing so severely limits the benefits of conducting survey research online. One of the issues with emailed surveys is that there can be conflicts between versions of word processing programs, making it difficult or impossible for a participant to open and/or complete the survey. If the survey is included in the body of an email, the format can be altered, causing questions to appear strange to the person completing the survey and adding extraneous symbols (e.g. ?, >, and *). All of the data gathered still need to be cleaned and prepared for analysis much like data collected offline.

Creating a web-based survey instrument mitigates many of the downsides to emailing a survey. The instrument, for example, will appear the same to all participants in its formatting, images, coloring and so forth (Mann & Stewart, 2000). It's also possible to format responses with check boxes ☐, radio buttons ○, and text boxes ⬚⬚⬚ for short-answer questions, making it significantly easier for people to provide answers. Analysis is much easier as well, given that the instruments are formatted consistently and, typically, there is a back-end database collecting all of the response data.

The limitations of choosing a web-based survey model for your research are relatively obvious. The first is the need for technical skill. Survey sites are built as a progression of HTML web pages containing a number of form items for the user to respond to questions via text fields, check boxes, multiple choice buttons and perhaps sliders. The interaction is via CGI and thus survey sites are usually built with the usual dynamic web scripting tools, very often with PHP. The returned data is stored on the server, usually in a database system. The technology required is quite similar to that which enables blogs and wikis. Formatting a survey takes time and skill. It also requires some type of hosting environment such as an institutional server or an ISP (Internet Service Provider). In addition to the web programming (in PHP for instance) and database skills necessary for constructing the survey instrument, it is necessary to be comfortable using FTP (File Transfer Protocol), or other methods, for uploading your files on to your host server and downloading data as they are acquired. In some instances, though, the need for manual (FTP) downloads can be avoided by the use of a script to automate data downloads. If the technical skills noted need to be acquired, keep in mind that you will require a budget for that support.

If you are debating which way to go with your research, we hope that budget expenses for technical skills will not be the primary deciding factor. Keep in mind that other types of surveys would involve mailing costs, copying services, paper expense, and the staff to input data. Even if surveys are emailed, someone has to clean up the data and prepare them for analysis. Therefore, we encourage you to consider the expense of technical skills for survey development or for using an online service simply as a shift in expense from one mode of researching to another. Rather than a decision based on budgetary constraints, the more important considerations are those which will enable you to be successful in your study, facilitating the best access to the best data for your particular research effort.

Technical specifics

Web-based surveys can be run from a hosted site, or from a server belonging to the researcher. Online surveys are, technologically speaking, presented as entry forms to a database, so a network-enabled (and preferably web-enabled) database application such as the **FileMaker** pro application is one way to do it. It has a forms editor which can be used to build the survey; and the responses are stored directly in the FileMaker database, which can be accessed and reports generated using built-in tools. When creating a new file, Filemaker presents a dialog to create a field.

The type of field can be text, numbers, dates or containers. To create an input field with check boxes or radio buttons, which are useful to limit the possible inputs, the field has first to be created, and then modified with the Format->Field Control->Set Up menu.

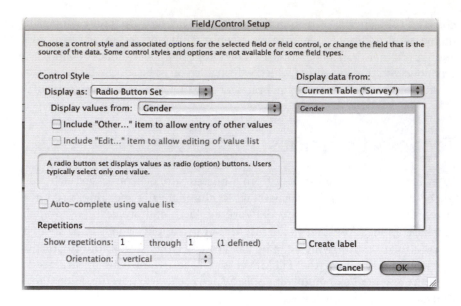

This process is repeated for each question. The survey can then be web-enabled to make it available to the public. As a full-fledged database application, FileMaker has many tools for creating reports and summaries of the collected data. However, running surveys with FileMaker currently has a few drawbacks which make it a bit more difficult to use than some other options. FileMaker's form entry mode shows one table on a page. If, as is commonly the case, the survey is to be represented as multiple pages, then multiple tables will need to be created, and a scripted button will have to be created to allow the survey taker to move on to the next page. Currently, the web view of FileMaker databases is designed to mimic the direct view when using the application, and is not completely suitable as an interface to people taking a survey, who should have no interests in the specifics of a database. Older versions of FileMaker had a web mark-up language to help design the web form, but this feature was dropped in version 6. However FileMaker version 9 will have a PHP application programming interface (API), which will make it easier to design the web-based view presented to end-users.

Otherwise, online surveys can be built entirely using open source or, at any rate, freely available tools. Open source software in general means software that can be downloaded and modified by the user, subject to certain restrictions. Open source often means free of cost, but that is not necessarily the case. Someone with good skills in database management and web application programming could create a web-based survey from scratch using open source tools such as the **Apache** web server, **Mysql** or **Postgresql** database systems, and web scripting languages such as PHP, perl, python or ruby, or in a somewhat different approach with the Java programming language. Fortunately for most researchers, there are freeware packages where most of the work has been done for you. For example **phpESP** (the PHP Easy Survey Processor) from Butterfat LLC, which is hosted at SourceForge (sourceforge.net/projects/phpesp), can be easily downloaded. Creating the content in phpESP is straightforward, and there is a demo at the site. The following shows a few screen shots from a session at the demo site. It starts with the management interface.

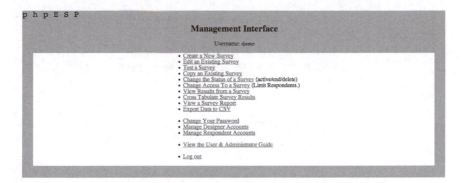

We'll go on to create a new survey, but looking at the menu, we can see that phpESP has a few convenient ways to report results from finished surveys as well.

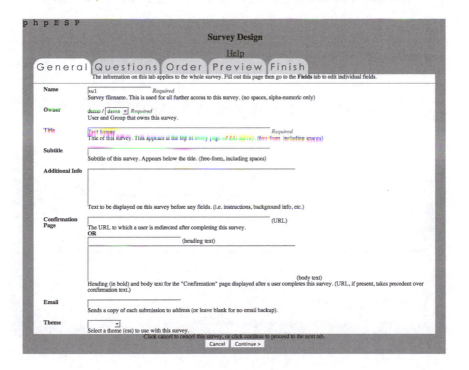

In the initial design page, we give the survey a name and title. From there we create some questions – in this example three questions on two screens. The first question will be to select gender, given two choices supplied by radio buttons.

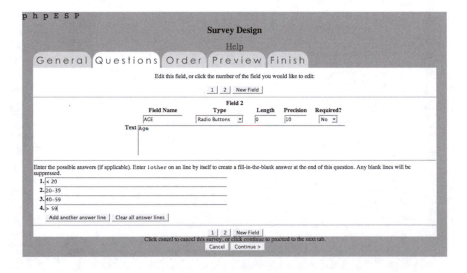

The second question will be to describe your age from a set of ranges, again using radio buttons.

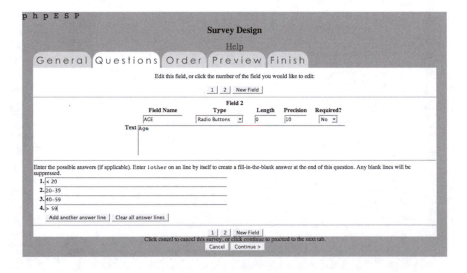

And the third and last page will be to offer an opinion by selecting one or more categories from check boxes.

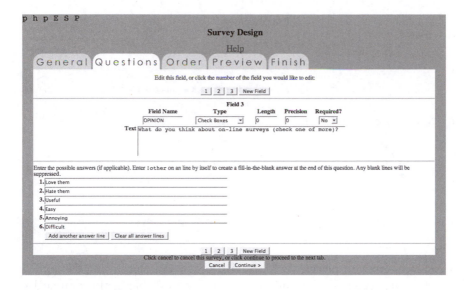

Now we'll review the order of the questions. We've added a section break between questions 2 and 3, which will cause the third question to appear on a second web page to the survey taker.

Continuing from there, we return to the management page and either test or activate the survey. A survey taker going the web site will see the following two web pages (with example answers supplied).

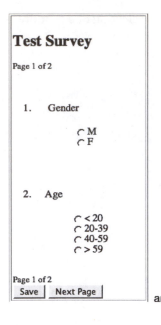

and

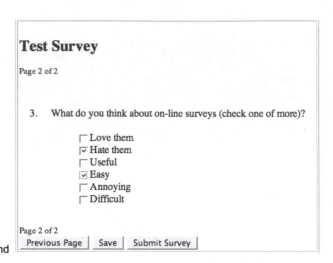

The survey-creation process is made fairly easy. One limitation to phpESP is that the input categories are limited to what is available in the standard web page input form, which includes text boxes, radio buttons, check boxes and drop-down menus, but does not include sliders and other continuously variable selectors, which might be useful in some circumstances.

In addition to freeware tools, there are commercial survey tools that can be installed on a web server, such as the **Survey** application from Educara Software (www.educara.com/educara.cgi/products). This will have a somewhat more sophisticated looking presentation to the survey taker, but works in almost the same way as phpESP. Both phpESP and Survey require a functioning web server and database system for storage. While administering a web server in this context or any other is not too hard to do, it raises a few issues for a researcher. If the web server is owned by and/or managed on an institutional network, then the institution is likely to have network access restrictions that will need to be addressed. Most often this amounts to requesting that the HTTP network port (port 80) for the server be made accessible to the outside world through any firewalls. If the web server is hosted on a home network, you will need to ensure that the Internet Service Provider (ISP) allows web servers to be running from your home. If they do, then you will need to determine whether or not there are any restrictions on network traffic that would constrain your research effort. In either case, web servers are often targets for malware hackers. Unfortunately there are people who, for a variety of reasons, scan the internet for web sites with software weaknesses that they can exploit. This usually means that they are able to bypass the security of the web site and install their own programs, which might then be used by them to do further scans, or perhaps to send spam mail.

Operators of web sites need to ensure that software is kept up to date, and access rules are restricted to an appropriate level. Log files need to be checked periodically to see who is accessing the web site, and the hosting computer needs to be monitored for unauthorized software.

Alternatively, instead of developing an online survey on your own, an easier and sometimes more cost-effective route is to use an online survey service. Using a service eliminates the need to manage a web server and database; but it also limits your access to the data to whatever method is provided by the service. There are many services and these services expand every day. Arguably, the best place to begin is to do an online search for online survey providers. At present, there are services such as Psychdata (www.psychdata.net) that are designed to meet the needs of a specific research community (in this case, Psychology researchers).

Random Stimulus Assignment
(within a survey)

Random Stimulus Assignment allows you to present 1 of X stimuli (text, images or links to other files) to each participant who takes your survey. The system automatically records (in your survey data) which stimulus was presented to each participant.

Here's how it looks in the Survey Editor:

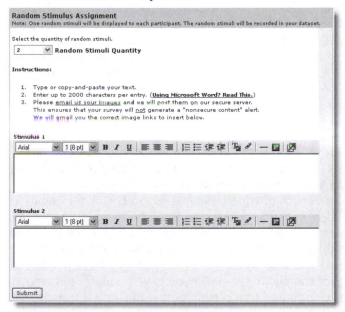

*an illustration from https://www.psychdata.com

In other cases, there are more general services available such as SurveyPro (www.surveypro.com), SurveyMonkey (www.surveymonkey.com) and SurveySaid (www.surveysaid.com). Some are designed for a corporate market, some are more academically oriented, and others are more general for a broad audience. Some allow you to purchase a basic subscription while others require an institutional license for use. Issues to consider when evaluating an online survey service provider are listed in the following box.

Tips 'n Tricks

Evaluating web-based survey service providers

- How does the application service provider license use of their application? Do they charge a basic fee by number of questions in a survey, number of surveys administered, by how long a study runs, or by the number of participants in a study?
- Do they limit the number of participants who can take your survey? What happens when you reach their limit?
- Do they limit how long the survey can run on their service? If so, when does the time limit begin?
- Is the application easy to use and intuitive in how it is designed for use?
- What are the data storage options (and how do you access your data during the study)?
- Will your survey appear online with banner advertisements or can they be eliminated? (Banner ads are those blocks that appear on the sides, top and bottom of a page advertising a product or service when accessing a web page. Many service providers keep their prices low for the user by selling banner advertisement space on their site.)
- How much flexibility does the program allow for survey customization? Can you change the background? Fonts? Colors? Insert images? Create an if/then algorithm to branch participants into different tracks in a study?
- Are there any tools available for viewing your findings, especially graphically, or is visual review of your findings only available after downloading data into another application?
- Does the vendor provide technical support? Online? Email? Telephone? Is it included in the service or will you be assessed a fee each time you access assistance? Is the phone number an "800," or is it a standard area code (which for some users can be problematic if left on hold or having to work their way through a system to get to a person, all the while paying for the phone time)? Do you have an unlimited amount of support time or is it limited to a certain period of time? Is it available 24 hours or during a particular time period (in a particular time zone)?

Although working through the preceding types of questions when selecting an online survey vendor may limit poor selections and costly mistakes, there are no guarantees – just as there are no guarantees that mailing a survey to a set list of participants will provide an adequate and appropriate response rate for analysis. We can say with confidence, however, that being clear about expectations and resources will make the process go much more smoothly and minimize the potential for major problems in a study.

In this chapter we have attempted to give you a general overview of survey techniques, and how they apply to the web-based environment. It was our intention to provide you with general tools to think about web-based survey options and begin to develop your own ideas about what will work best for you and your research endeavors. As in early chapters, once you have an idea of which approach you're going to take, and have begun to outline your study with the tools provided here, we encourage you to look for manuals and online help services that will enable you to become comfortable within the specific environment in which you're planning to work.

7 THE WORLD OF WEB 2.0: BLOGS, WIKIS AND WEBSITES

Chapter summary

- Interactive web sites have enabled an enormous growth of user-generated web content.
- Blogs tell an individual's story; they're typically a monologue that allows for an occasional question or comment, as opposed to open interaction.
- Wikis are multi-user web site editors, which is why they are a popular collaboration tool.

In the following pages we'll discuss the basics of web sites, weblogs (blogs) and wikis, and the ways in which they are being used for research purposes. In previous chapters we discussed technologies that allow users to send and receive information to and from a specific list of addressees. Web technology is different from email and messaging in that a document is published on the web and viewers themselves make the decision whether to access it. In the context of this book, the web is interesting in that it is both a medium for distributing information and a seemingly infinite source of data to research.

In its earlier days, that is, before roughly the year 2000, the web was mostly a publishing tool. Web servers were mostly in-house or at a commercial web service provider. A certain level of expertise was required to operate the web server and also to generate web content. Recent combinations of increasing network speeds, huge increases in disk storage capacity and software to ease the creation of web sites and web content, have made possible sites such as **MySpace**, **Facebook**, **YouTube**, **flickr** and ones like them, as well as blog and wiki sites. This has made it much easier for the average person (with access to a computer and the Internet) to express him or herself to a world-wide audience without having to go through a mediator such as a magazine or book publisher, or a television or radio station. This has empowered people, and is changing the relationship between commercial providers and consumers as all such people can now be providers as well as consumers (Wikinomics: Tapscott and Williams, 2006). A code word for this new use of the World Wide Web is Web 2.0, which describes "this trend to enhance creativity, information sharing, and, most notably, collaboration among users" (http://en.wikipedia.org/wiki/Web_2.0, accessed on 6 May 2008). Of course, not all consumer-generated content is accurate or worthwhile, but then neither is all commercial content. The interactive web is in the process of significantly changing the nature of several industries, among them news, music, television and politics. These are all interesting areas for social science inquiry.

Most people today have some familiarity with website development, so we'll be brief. There are many ways to go about it. From most basic to more advanced, one can create the web documents by directly writing the HTML (HyperText Markup Language) code with a text editor, and transferring the document files to the web server document area. One can use web site editors such as **Adobe Dreamweaver** or **Mozilla SeaMonkey** to create the web content in a graphical WYSIWYG fashion, meaning that what you see on the screen is what you get when you print, and then transfer the file to the web server. Or finally the web site can be set up with a Content Management System (CMS), which is software on the web server that manages a whole web site. Contributors to the web site log in to the system, and are given access to some or all of the web site documents and, depending on permissions, are allowed to create and or update documents on the server. Examples of Content Management Systems are **Drupal**, **MediaWiki** and **Microsoft SharePoint**. All the big social networking sites like MySpace and Facebook are made possible by some type of CMS. The essential pieces of a content management system are an authentication system, a visual web document editor, and a storage scheme, which hides the actual form and location of documents from the user, and which is usually a relational database management system (RDBMS). A relational database is of interest to a researcher when he or she wants to retrieve content from a web site that he or she has access to. RDBMSs will be described in more detail in Chapter 8.

Weblogs (blogs)

A particular form of user-generated web site is called a weblog or, in short, a blog. Blogs are web sites where an author creates documents such as diaries or commentary at (hopefully) regular intervals. Usually the author allows viewers of the site to post comments about the document, or engage in some type of online discussion. Subjects range from politics (e.g. www.democratic-conversation.com or dailykos.com) to personal and life events (e.g. www.triplebranch.blogspot.com) to consumer gadgets (e.g. gizmodo.com). Blogs often include images as well as text and dynamically link to other blogs and sites on the Internet. By convention, articles or posts are placed in reverse chronological order, that is, the most recent is at the top. Also by convention, articles once posted, are not changed, though errata may certainly be posted later.

As Torill Elvira Mortensen notes, "the literature on weblogs is somewhat elusive, because the subject (weblogs), the academic publishing about weblogs, and both the academic and popular discussions about weblogs take place, to an extremely high extent, on the Internet" (in Coiro et al., 2008: 451). The practice of blogging itself is a "process of self-definition and a way of inscribing the individual on the global Net" (ibid.).

The characteristic of blog sites is that it is very easy for the author to create new content. So their usage is growing phenomenally. There are currently tens of millions of blog sites world-wide and more than a million articles are posted each day. Posting on a blog is less daunting to many people than writing a paper; partly because there is no editor (or teacher) to critique it, so blogs are often a way, particularly for young people, to exercise their literacy (Penrod, 2007). If there is a comment section to the blog, and if visitors to the blog use it, then that is a way for the author to get feedback, but it feels more like peer criticism than authoritarian criticism.

Blogs provide a significant amount of personal data. This is one of the reasons researchers find them of interest. Blogs represent easily accessible qualitative data for a researcher. While not necessarily focused on a particular topic, it can provide formidable data. It is important to note, however, that blogging is beginning to be questioned *as a means of* surveillance (Staples, 2000). Users place their personal data online, making these widely available to friend and foe. Whether or not people will continue to blog truthfully, whether they will reveal as much as they currently do, or whether it will evolve into a fictitious genre remains to be seen. For researchers, it is important to be clear for what purpose a blog is being used and in what ways the data might be misleading or intentionally fictitious.

Blogs, for example, have become the bane of a journalist's world in that they have made any 15-year-old child into new competition, providing a soap box for any and all opinions (Mortensen in Coiro et al., 2008). Editors note that it is difficult to remain on top of key stories, because blogs have enabled "netizens" to scoop the biggest stories. In a similar fashion, many anticipate that wikis will become the collaborative workspace of tomorrow, making them a part of corporate life. As they become a routine work tool, they will evolve into many other uses.

As a research tool, blogs represent qualitative data. They lend themselves to narrative and content analysis techniques specifically. In most cases, cutting and pasting is the easiest way to capture data for storage and analysis.

Example
SAMPLE BLOG

March 08, 2007
Identity Politics Gone Wild

First we had the strikingly pale Bill Clinton proclaimed as America's First Black President by Toni Morrison as an odd reward for pandering to identity politics. Now, the *New York Sun* reports that the First Woman President may well *have a Y chromosome*, if John Edwards wins the White House:

Toni Morrison famously dubbed President Clinton America's "first black president." With that barrier broken, the comments of a prominent feminist are provoking debate about who may lay a similar claim to the title of America's first woman president.

The candidate being touted as a torchbearer for women is not Senator Clinton, but one of her former colleagues, John Edwards. At a rally near the University of California, Berkeley campus this week, a veteran of the abortion-rights movement, Kate Michelman, asked and answered the question she gets most frequently about her decision to back the male former senator from North Carolina.

"Why John Edwards, given the historic nature of our extraordinary campaign for the presidency this year with Hillary Clinton and Barack Obama and all the others?" Ms Michelman asked as she warmed up the crowd for Mr Edwards. "I've gotten to know a lot of political leaders over the years that I've been an advocate for women's rights. I know the difference between those who advocate as a political position and those who understand the reality of women's lives."

Compared to Mrs Clinton, Mr Edwards is short an "X" chromosome, but listening to Ms Michelman, that is easy to forget. "As a lawyer, as a senator, as a husband, as a father of two daughters, he understands the reality of women's lives. He understands the centrality of women's lives and experience to the health and well-being of society as a whole. ... He understands that on an extremely personal level," she said.

Quite frankly, it shouldn't matter which chromosomes or skin pigmentation a candidate has on an individual basis. In a general sense, we want to ensure that the political process remains open to everyone,

(Continued)

and diversity among elected officials gives us an indication of whether we're successful at it. If diversity is a goal in and of itself, as the Toni Morrisons and Kate Michelmans have argued in the past, then granting honorary minority status on rich, white men seems to be counter-productive.

It points out the silliness of identity politics in a comic way, as the final stage of the process. Identity becomes so much more important than actual policy that candidates have to assume ridiculous poses as the most female of all candidates in a race, even while the race includes actual females and the claimant is a male. In Bill Clinton's case, the appelation belies the fact that actual black men and women ran for the office before he did, and did not win the nomination — and that he's not really black.

The first black president will be the candidate of African descent who wins the most Electoral College votes. The first female president will be the candidate with two X chromosomes who takes the oath of office on January 20 of the given year. Perhaps the Democrats might dispense with the gender and ethnic politics and just focus on policy instead.

Sphere It ⬚ ⬚DIGG IT!⬚ *1 blog reaction*
Posted by Ed Morrissey at March 8, 2007 06:02 AM

Listed below are links to weblogs that reference *Identity Politics Gone Wild*:

» *Thank You, Captain Ed* from Growing Old Disgracefully

All I hear in the discussions of the candidates is whether "Hillary is feminine enough" or whether Obama "is black enough". I still don't know Obama's foreign policy stance. I still don't know what or if Hillar ... [*Read More*]

Tracked on March 8, 2007 08:22 AM

>Comments

"As a lawyer, as a senator, as a husband, as a father of two daughters, he understands the reality of women's lives. He understands the centrality of women's lives and experience to the health and well-being of society as a whole. ... He understands that on an extremely personal level," she said.

Coming so soon after Ann Coulter's remark, this is just tooooo good. If only Michelman had added "the importance of good hair" to her list of things that Edwards "understands"...

Posted by: docjim505 🐚 at March 8, 2007 06:38 AM

Now, what if that wannabe transgender City Manager in Florida goes on to bigger and better things? Could he/she be the "first woman president" if elected?

Posted by: BarCodeKing 🐚 at March 8, 2007 07:13 AM

"Perhaps the Democrats might dispense with the gender and ethnic politics and just focus on policy instead."

If properly explained, the Democrat policy is wildly unpopular with the electorate, which is why they resort to this sort of sham, hocus pocus redirection, rather than discussing what they actually want to accomplish (socialized everything), once elected.

Posted by: NoDonkey 🐚 at March 8, 2007 07:18 AM

Of course, Ms Michelman would probably be aghast at a Condi presidential run — even though she's both black and a woman.

And Mr Edwards, being identified as the "woman" presidential candidate won't help you.

Posted by: rbj 🐚 at March 8, 2007 07:22 AM

http://www.captainsquartersblog.com/mt/archives/009354.php, accessed on 8 March 2007

The preceding blog is fairly typical. It demonstrates a substantive, authored editorial on the topic of identity politics. It is then followed by a discussion with shorter contributions that reflect a kind of public dialog or debate. This type of data is useful for political analysis or other types of social science research. Managing the content for analysis in a program such as HyperResearch simply requires cutting and pasting the text into a word processor document file and inserting a tilde (~) between sections to enable the researcher to code each submission independently. If you have access to the content management system's back-end database on the blog server, then you can extract the posting and comments from the database with database tools. This may be preferable for large quantities of text, making it easier to prepare for analysis.

One of the challenges of the blogosphere is the sheer quantity of blogs. There are volumes of blogs in a number of different languages. Most researchers, therefore, will want to take advantage of some kind of service for assisting with their search for quality data, as well as managing the volumes of blogs they want to use in their research. One such service is Technorati. By their own statistics, Technorati (www.technorati.com) tracks over 112.8 million blogs and over 250 million pieces of tagged social media. As they note on their information site, "bloggers frequently link to and comment on other blogs, creating the type of immediate connection one would have in a conversation." Their service tracks these links, indexing tens of thousands of updates every hour. According to Technorati data, there are over 175,000 new blogs every day. Bloggers update their blogs regularly to the tune of over 1.6 million posts per day, or over 18 updates a second.

In addition to management tools, there are a number of search engines. One of the better search services is IceRocket (www.icerocket.com). It has a variety of criteria by which to search and various means by which to list a blog. Blogarama (http://www.blogarama.com/) lists over 82,000 sites to date, organized by subject heading, which points to another type of service. Some services are helpful for organizational purposes, enabling a user to track blogs and their usage. One such service is del.icio.us, enabling users to organize and manage websites, blogs, and so forth, in a bookmark fashion similar to the way in which people are used to managing websites in a web browser.

In addition to capturing, organizing and analyzing data in existing blogs, a researcher could choose to create a blog. In the interactive environment of a blog, a researcher could manage a type of focus group by raising questions and challenging participants by responding to submissions. (Again, note the exchange in the example). Much like other electronic focus groups, this form of research presents challenges for focus group moderators (Gaiser, 1997). For example, it would be difficult in a blog setting for the moderator to have much control over the discussion, making it difficult to keep people on a particular task or discussion thread. Some researchers may be concerned about researcher bias, with so much authored information being the beginning of a discussion thread. The blog could present a kind of double-edged sword. Without substantial initial enticement to engage, participants may provide little follow-up, limiting the benefit of the blog environment for data collection. On the other hand, too much researcher involvement up front raises the issues of research bias. Lori Kendall notes, however, that "participant observation allows researchers to gain a better understanding of participants' ranges of identity performances and the meaning those performances have for them," suggesting that concern about researcher bias through participation in the study may be unfounded in online research (1999: 71). Regardless of any moderator challenges, however, researchers should not be deterred from attempting actively to capture the rich data accessible in a blog environment.

As with other internet technologies, blogs may be hosted on a personal web server or one belonging to your institution. This requires a working and accessible web server and blog management software, such as WordPress (wordpress.com), TypePad (www.typepad.com) or Moveable Type (www.moveabletype.org). Blogs may also be hosted on a blog service, possibly using one of these same software management systems. Some of the biggest free (meaning advertiser-supported) hosted sites are Blogger (www.blogger.com) and Blogsome (www.blogsome.com). The social networking sites MySpace and Facebook also provide blogging facilities.

In every case, the author interacts with their blog through his or her web browser, and the procedure is fairly similar. Creating an account and a blog site on blogger.com is described in great detail in Sauers (2006). The main points are visiting the blogger.com site to first create an account, which is a Google account (and allows access to other Google services). Then you choose a name for your blog and a template which controls the appearance of the blog site. Once the blog site is successfully created, you can create posts. You may either compose in raw HTML, or create with a visual editor. Among the many other options that can be controlled, are whether other contributors can create posts on the blog, whether or not comments will be moderated, and how often posts get moved off the main page and into the archived section.

Wikis

Wikis are similar to blogs in that they are user-generated web sites, but differ in that the document itself is allowed to be modified by multiple authorized users of the wiki site; it is a way of collaboratively creating and editing a document. A wiki is typically not a simple document like a journal article, but is often a complete website with different pages linked together. Wikis are generally not aimed at the general public, but are more often for the internal storage display of accumulated knowledge, and are therefore usually not fancy looking, but there is no reason they cannot be visually attractive. The name "wiki" comes from the Hawaiian word for fast, and is named after the Wikiwiki Shuttle at the Honolulu Airport.

The grand-daddy wiki is, of course, Wikipedia (www.wikipedia.com), an enormous collection of user-contributed knowledge. Anyone may request a log-in to Wikipedia and create an entry; there are currently over a million registered users. It is this openness that has made Wikipedia such a wide resource. There are some controls to limit vandalism of the site, but mostly the fact that every entry can be reviewed and edited by others generally pushes all entries towards greater accuracy. Comparisons between Wikipedia and standard encyclopedias show similar levels of errors (Giles, 2005). The advantage of Wikipedia is that, even if the errors are more frequent or greater, they will also be fixed more quickly in all likelihood.

The server technology behind wikis is the same as for blog sites. They require a log-in authorization system, graphically oriented web page editor, and a content management system, including a database back-end for information storage. Some wiki management products are MediaWiki (www.mediawiki.org/wiki/MediaWiki) (used by Wikipedia), and MoinMoin (moinmoin.wiki wikiweb.de). Wikis do not generally have fancy visual editors, but rely on a simplified mark-up language to create web pages that include a subset of the full capability of HTML mark-up.

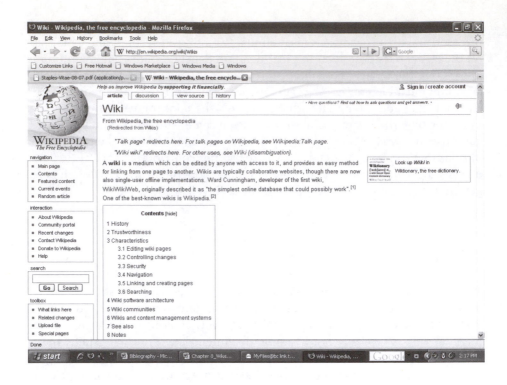

Wikis are far less prevalent than blogs, perhaps because they seem more like work than play, and they have a more specific purpose, so there are fewer hosting sites for wikis. Among the ones that exist are Wikia (wikia.com) and WetPaint (wetpaint.com). It is also harder to search for wikis than blogs. One way is to use the Wiki Bus Tour, which can be started at http://en.wikipedia.org/wiki/Wikipedia:TourBusStop.

Feeds and syndication

The very large number of blogs and dynamic web sites that are out there present a problem to researchers wishing to keep track of them. Certainly, web browsers have a bookmark feature that allows a browser to return quickly to a desired site, but it still requires the viewer to explicitly select the bookmark and go there. Increasingly, therefore, blog sites and other sites with frequently changing content provide what is called a "feed". More accurately such a web or blog page has a link on it which points to a special document, written in a form of Extensible Markup Language (XML) which can be imported by a feed reader or aggregator. These reader applications, with this information, know to check the web site automatically for new content and, if there is something new, present it to the viewer. There are a few different languages that provide the feed information: RSS which stands for one or all of Rich Site Summary, Really Simple Syndication or RDF Site Summary, and comes in several not entirely compatible versions, and also a separate language called Atom. But they are all dialects of XML and, for most people, what is in the feed link document does not actually matter; most feed readers will know what to do with any of them.

To provide a feed, the blog page or web page will usually display an icon that the user can click, either to get information about the feed, or actually to subscribe to the feed. These icons may vary, but are usually orange, and may contain "RSS", "Atom", "RDF" or "XML". Additionally, modern browsers, including the latest version of each of Firefox, Internet Explorer, Safari and Opera, will detect the presence of a feed link, and put an orange icon like into the address field. Clicking on this icon will have different effects on different browsers. Firefox opens a window displaying the site in feed form, and gives the user an option of methods to subscribe. The "Live Bookmarks" option creates a feed icon in the tool bar, and subsequent articles from this site will appear there. It also gives the option of subscribing through a different application, which may be an email and news reader like Thunderbird, Office Outlook or Windows Mail. In a mail or news tool, the latest feeds will appear just as an unread email or news item, and can be marked or categorized in the various ways that mail tools are able. Lastly, Firefox gives the option of subscribing through Google or Yahoo, which may be useful if you use those sites as portals, and through the Bloglines (bloglines.com) site, which is a web site designed specifically for organizing feeds. Bloglines requires a free account, but has useful tools for organizing feeds. The other browsers – Internet Explorer, Opera and Safari – subscribe to feeds within the application itself. However, one last option is to find the feed icon in the document itself, not the one in the tool bar, and choose "copy link location", which is usually available in the mouse right-click option. The link location will be a URL pointing to an XML file. Then in the mail application, we will use Thunderbird as an example, select a new account of type "RSS News & Blogs". Then select "Manage Subscriptions", then "Add", and paste in the URL and select "OK". Your mail application will then be subscribed to this site's feeds.

Feeds are typically mostly text, but may in fact consist of audio and/or video, in which case they are known as Podcasts. The Apple iTunes application can be used to subscribe to audio and video feeds, and can save the feed to an iPod, hence the name. However, many applications that can present digital sound, like MP3 players, can play podcasts.

We end this chapter with a few notes on what a researcher needs to understand, should he or she wish to host a web site. Operating your own wiki or blog may be an attractive option for collecting data. However, running an interactive web site like a wiki or blog requires managing a web site with scripting enabled. This creates potential security vulnerabilities that your respective IT organization may resist. A decision will need to be made on who ensures the maximum possible security of the web server, including keeping up to date with patches, and also who repairs the damage in the event the server becomes compromised (see the section on Service Level Agreements in Chapter 2).

While relatively new to the world of research, wikis and blogs offer new opportunities for interacting with people on the web and gathering data. They need further exploration in regard to the value of the data generated in these environments. Currently, however, there are data and plenty of opportunity. It is our hope that these pages will inspire some to give them a try.

8 ACCESSING AND USING WEB-BASED DATA

Chapter summary

- A database can be any file or group of files that stores structured data.
- To the surprise of some, blogs and wikis are often built into databases.
- It is helpful to know how a relational database functions when preparing to perform data analysis.
- It is wise to do a complete assessment before downloading any online data.

There are endless variations on the type and format of data available to the researcher. Data may be created by the researcher or may have been collected previously by other researchers or some agency. Some data are explicitly entered into a computer by the researcher, some are stored automatically by a data collection application. In this chapter, we will examine a few different types of data and how they are represented; we will look at some issues with receiving data from other sources; and we will also describe how to protect and restrict access to stored data.

At one level, data can be considered quantitative or qualitative (also referred to as structured and unstructured). Structured data are data that have numerical values or are represented as categories. Unstructured data are typically documents or audio or video streams which have not been reduced or processed.

Whether quantitative or qualitative, data are stored as files on computers, and there are many ways to do so. In the simplest format, character and number data can be stored in text files, with no formatting information other than the end-of-line marker. In software parlance, structured and unstructured have a slightly different meaning from that described in the previous paragraph. A structured data file is one that has internal information on how the data are to be represented. An example of a structured data file is a spreadsheet. The file itself contains information about the rows, columns and cells and knows how to represent the data values within, whether they are numbers, text or dates, etc. A plain text file is generally considered to be an unstructured data file, even if it contains structured data in the earlier sense, because there is nothing in the file itself that describes how the information is structured. Other types of data might be log files or mail message stores, and these will usually be text files. Data collection applications write data either as raw text files or, quite often, into a relational database.

Unstructured files

Unstructured files are plain text files that are not directly associated with a specific application. The data in unstructured files may or may not be presented in a column format. If it is columnar, then there is some convention to define the columns. It may be that fields (or variables or columns) are separated from each other by a tab character (called tab separated), or the fields may be separated by a comma or other punctuation character (called comma separated), or the fields may be defined by their fixed width. Fixed-width field files are usually output by data collection applications, and are somewhat of a left-over from the old days of punch-card data storage, where data space was very limited and needed to be used as efficiently as possible.

Often data will be supplied in unstructured text files, but will also have an associated document, sometimes called a codebook, that describes how the text is to be interpreted as data. The following example illustrates a typical codebook. Note, for example, that a "2" in the code column for question #4 means that the participant was married sometime during the months of April to June. More specifically, the "29" before it in the frequency column indicates that 29 study participants were married sometime during the months of April to June. In this way, the codebook gives meaning to the numbers in a dataset.

Examples: AFDA Study Code book

In Home Questionnaire Code Book II, S.1

Frequency Code		Response	Variable Name	Type/ Length
If AGE ≥ 15, ask Q.3-5.				
3. Since {MOLE}, did you get married?			**H2GI3**	num 1
12031	0	*no [skip to Q.5]*		
97	1	yes		
2610	7	legitimate skip *[R<15 or age not given]*		

4. In what month [and year] did you get married?		**H2GI4M**	num 2
17	1	January to March	
29	2	April to June	
26	3	July to September	
25	4	October to December	
14641	97	legitimate skip [R *did not get married since {MOLI}*]	

4. In what [month and] year did you get married?		**H2GI4Y**	num 3
57	95	95	
40	96	96	
14641	997	legitimate skip [R *did not get married since {MOLI}*]	

5. What is your current marital status?		**H2GI5**	num 1
11996	1	not married	
123	2	married	
2610	7	legitimate skip [R*<15 or age not given*]	
9	8	don't know	

6. *[If SCHOOL YEAR]* Are you presently in school? *[If SUMMER]* Were you in school during this past school year?		**H2GI6**	num 1
998	0	no *[skip to Q.10]*	
8263	1	*yes [If summer, interviewer probe: Was that for the entire school year, or just part?]*	
5127	2	yes, the entire school year	
349	3	yes, part of the school year *[skip to Q.10]*	
1	8	don't know *[skip to Q.15]*	

7. {ARE/WERE} you attending {SAMPLE SCHOOL}?		**H2GI7**	num 1
3303	0	no *[skip to Q.9 if {SAMPLE SCHOOL} = {SISTER SCHOOL}]*	

HOME2CBK/MARSB

The box shows the first page of the codebook. It describes the name of the variable, its type (numerical), its width in characters, the meaning of the coded values, and permissible values.

* American Family Data Archive proprietary data set of Sociometrics Corp. (www.socio.com)

With this type of data, the researcher will usually want to convert the raw text file into a structured file such as a spreadsheet or an SAS or SPSS data file using the rules of the codebook. Data analysis applications like **SAS** and **SPSS** and the main spreadsheet applications like **MS Excel** and **OpenOffice Calc** have wizards to help import data (see also Chapter 9). Sometimes people will, by habit, use a word processing application to edit unstructured text files, but it is usually a bad idea to convert these unstructured files into a word processing application format like MS Word DOC format because the format adds information to the file which may prevent it from being interpreted properly by applications. On Windows, for example, text file should be edited if necessary with the Notepad accessory rather than Word. The Mac and Linux systems have default text editors. If the file is only for viewing by a user and not an application, however, then there is no problem in converting it to a word processing format.

Spreadsheet files

Much data are inherently organized as rows and columns. In a survey summary, for example, each row of data will correspond to an individual respondent, and each column will correspond to the responses to a given question. Spreadsheets are a very common and convenient way to store data that is column or field oriented. This is because the spreadsheet application implicitly understands the columns, and has facilities for easily selecting and manipulating values by column or by row. With a spreadsheet application it is easy to enter the information into the proper cell, so spreadsheet applications are often the first choice for researchers entering their own data at the keyboard. It should be noted that the field formatting information is specific to each spreadsheet application so spreadsheet files are not necessarily readable by applications other than the one that created them. However, **OpenOffice Calc** and many of the others are able to read MS Excel spreadsheets (XLS format) at least up to the 2003 format.

Spreadsheet applications usually include some analytical functionality as well. In some cases that is quite sufficient for analyzing the data. In other cases the data will be read into a more sophistical application. As a rule, though, data should be cleaned prior to placing them in an analytical application. Statistical and qualitative software applications are designed for analysis, not editing. As such, general editing is easier to complete in a spreadsheet with Excel or Calc. MS Excel is easy to work with for editing and is also fairly compatible with other applications for importing and exporting data.

Database files

Dynamic web sites like blogs, or web sites which take user input like online surveys, often use database software, such as **MySQL**, **MS SQLServer** or **MS**

Access, as a storage mechanism. A database can be any file or group of files that stores structured data. Most typically, though, the term database is used to mean a relational database (RDB). Relational databases are composed of one or more tables (that is, data that can be stored as rows and columns), and tables may have links (relations) to other tables in the database. A huge variety of data is stored in such databases, but not all data are conveniently stored in rows and columns. A prime counter-example is hierarchical or nested data, which can be represented by leaves and branches in a tree graph, and there is no easy representation of that in terms of rows and columns. The relationships between data objects (a specifically defined term in computer science) are usefully represented as trees, and there are databases called object databases to store this type of data. XML files (more about these in a later chapter) are often used to represent object data, so object databases often store XML data and are often called XML databases. Directory data, used to control authentication and access to computer systems and networks, are also often stored this way.

Tabular data could be stored in a text file or in a spreadsheet, but typically specialized software with its own table formats is used to enable the insertion and retrieval of data into tables at higher access rates than are possible with a text file. Commonly used database software packages are **MySQL** (open source, Unix/Linux, Mac OSX, Windows), **Postgresql** (open source, Unix/Linux, Mac OSX), **MS SQLServer** (Microsoft, Windows), **MS Access** (Microsoft, Windows), **FileMaker** (FileMaker, Windows, Mac OSX) and **Oracle** (Oracle, Unix/Linux, Mac OSX, Windows). There are many other database managers – databases are a huge industry. Many of these database applications can be managed using Structured Query Language (SQL). This is a specialized functional language used to manage relational data. The language has been standardized so there is little variation between different systems. Some applications, notably **MS Access** and **FileMaker Pro,** however, do not have SQL interpreters, but instead rely on graphically oriented query wizards. In either case, having the data in a database format allows for very flexible searching, categorization and selection of the data.

Web applications like blogs and wikis are often built with a MySQL storage back-end, because MySQL can be downloaded and installed for free, performs well for data retrieval, and is relatively easy to manage. Dynamic sites that are hosted on Microsoft technology usually have SQLServer as a database back-end. FileMaker Pro server may also be a useful database back-end server. FileMaker Pro client (as opposed to the server version) and MS Access offer user-friendly interfaces to the data but are not typically suitable as back-end databases for applications. They may, however, be very useful in the analysis stage of the research.

Relational databases

The various applications that store data in RDBMSs generally provide tools at varying degrees of user-friendliness to retrieve the stored data and generate reports from them. On occasion, the researcher will find these tools too limiting, and will want to retrieve the data directly from the database. When that situation arises, the researcher will have to use the SQL language to access the database. This is the most general and flexible method to retrieve data from a database. We'll describe at some length the SQL language and explain how RDBMSs store and retrieve data, so that the user may understand how to access data in that format. There are many books that describe the SQL language in detail, one good example being Bowman, Emerson & Darnovsky (2001).

Example
Creating a database in MySQL with SQL

Relational databases consist of one or more tables, which in turn consist of rows and columns (which are also called records and fields). The columns are defined to be a particular data type: integers, floating point numbers, fixed length text, or variable length text. For example, let us imagine a database called FORUM. It consists of two tables, USERS and COMMENTS. The USERS table is used to store some information about users: their first and last name, their age, and an identifier which is used internally. The COMMENTS table is used to store a piece of text communicated by the user, the ID of the user in question, and the time of day of the comment. To create this database in SQL, would take the following commands:

```
CREATE DATABASE FORUM;
USE FORUM;
CREATE TABLE USERS (ID int auto_increment,
  FIRST varchar(255),
  LAST varchar(255),
  primary key (ID));
CREATE TABLE COMMENTS (USERID int,
  TIME timestamp,
  MESSAGE text);
```

The table creation command specifies the name of the field along with its data type. In our cases the data types are integers, variable length character strings, and time stamps. The "primary key" definition is an optimization that tells the software to search using the first (the ID) column. The database tables will be defined, but empty at this point. To review what was just created one would enter:

```
SHOW TABLES;

+ ——————————————— +
| Tables_in_project1     |
```

```
+ ——————————— +
| users              |
| comments           |
+ ——————————— +
```
2 rows in set (0.00 sec)
DESCRIBE USERS;
```
+ ——— + —————— + — + — + ——— + ————— +
| Field | Type         | Null | Key | Default | Extra          |
+ ——— + —————— + — + —— + ——— + ————— +
| ID    | int(11)      |      | PRI | NULL    | auto_increment |
| FIRST | varchar(255) | YES  |     | NULL    |                |
| LAST  | varchar(255) | YES  |     | NULL    |                |
+ ——— + —————— + — + — + ——— + ————— +
```
3 rows in set (0.15 sec)
DESCRIBE COMMENTS;
```
+ ————— + ————— + — + — + ——— + —— +
| Field   | Type          | Null | Key | Default | Extra |
+ ————— + ————— + — + — + ——— + —— +
| USERID  | int(11)       | YES  |     | NULL    |       |
| TIME    | timestamp(14) | YES  |     | NULL    |       |
| MESSAGE | text          | YES  |     | NULL    |       |
+ ————— + ————— + — + — + ——— + —— +
```
3 rows in set (0.00 sec)
Now we can enter a few values, first we define some users:
INSERT INTO USERS VALUES (null, 'Sam', 'Lam');
INSERT INTO USERS VALUES (null, 'Jean', 'Green');
Notice the value null in the first field; a value does not need to be provided here because the field was defined with AUTO_INCREMENT, and the DBMS takes care of assigning a sequentially increasing number for each new entry. To see that, we make a simple query:
SELECT * FROM USERS:
```
+ — + —— + —— +
| ID  | FIRST | LAST  |
+ — + —— + —— +
| 1   | Sam   | Lam   |
| 2   | Jean  | Green |
+ — + —— + —— +
```
2 rows in set (0.27 sec)
This operation selects all rows from the table and displays all columns of each row. See that Sam Lam has been automatically given the ID 1 and Jean Green has been given the ID 2. When we store their messages, we will use these ID numbers in place of their names:

INSERT INTO COMMENTS VALUES (1, null,

(Continued)

'Hello, I am Sam Lam, I am new to this forum');
INSERT INTO COMMENTS VALUES (2, null,
 'Greetings, my name is Jean Green, I just joined this forum');
INSERT INTO COMMENTS VALUES (1, null,
 'Hi Jean, I am also new, Sam')

The null value in the second field of this case will be filled by the current time when the message was inserted. Using the ID value saves table space because we don't need to store the full name of the user in each row of the COMMENTS table. We query the contents of this table:

```
SELECT * FROM COMMENTS;
+ ————— + ————————— + ———————————————————————————————
——————— +
| USERID | TIME | MESSAGE |
+ ————— + ————————— + ———————————————————————————————
——————— +
|        1 | 20070512221208 | Hello, I am Sam Lam, I am new to this forum |
|        2 | 20070512221255 | Greetings, my name is Jean Green, I just joined
this forum |
|        1 | 20070512221406 | Hi Jean, I am also new, Sam |
+ ————— + ————————— + ———————————————————————————————
——————— +
3 rows in set (0.04 sec)
```

With these two tables, we can do a slightly more complicated query to use the relational aspect of the database. The USERID field of the COMMENTS table is a relation into the USERS table via the ID field. We can do what is called a join to get a result that combines information from both tables:

```
SELECT    USERS.FIRST,USERS.LAST,COMMENTS.TIME,COMMENTS.MESSAGE
FROM USERS,COMMENTS WHERE USERS.ID = COMMENTS.USERID;
+ ————— + ————————— + ———————————————————————————————
——————— +
| FIRST | LAST | TIME | MESSAGE |
+ ————— + ————————— + ———————————————————————————————
——————— +
| Sam | Lam | 20070512221208 | Hello, I am Sam Lam, I am new to this
forum |
| Jean | Green | 20070512221255 | Greetings, my name is Jean Green, I just
joined this forum |
| Sam | Lam | 20070512221406 | Hi Jean, I am also new, Sam |
+ ————— + ————————— + ———————————————————————————————
——————— +
3 rows in set (0.42 sec)
```

Here you see that to join you need to figure out which username to use from the ID value. The more complicated notation using dots is required in this case because we are referring to multiple tables in the query; usually the table is implied. In addition to saving space, another reason to use indexes and joins or links instead of putting the username in each comment entry, is that it helps to keep the data consistent, preventing typo errors. This usage is called "normalization" in database theory. One of the main strategies for normalization is that any data item that appears more than once in a database, should be placed a single time in an appropriately separate table, and all references to that item should be via relations to that table. This ensures that all references to that item are exactly the same.

These examples provide you with a feel for how the SQL language works and interacts with databases, which will be useful to researchers needing a very high degree of control over the extraction of information from their databases. In practice, most databases will be created by some other software and will be presented to the researcher, so no table creation or row inserts will typically be done directly by the researcher. However, analysis of data in the databases will require extraction or querying of data from the database and this will be accomplished with the SELECT statements. There are many modifiers to the SELECT function that allow more sophisticated selections, but these can be learned with any guide to SQL. It may seem a bit daunting at first to learn a new specialized language, but for researchers who have a frequent need to create queries which may differ slightly or greatly, creating the queries in SQL becomes the fastest way to accomplish it.

Despite the previous paragraph, many users will still prefer a more graphical user interface to their data. **MS Access** and **FileMaker** provide built-in "wizards" to guide the user through creating queries and reports. These wizards are easier to learn for the casual user than the actual SQL language. **MySQL** does not include any graphical extraction tools itself, but there are other products provide the tools for MySQL databases; one such application is called phpMyAdmin (http://www.phpmyadmin.net/home_page/index.php). It is a web server based program that is written in the PHP language. The user uses a web browser to see an interface into the database.

Example
Creating a database with graphical forms and MS Access

Using the same extraction of data from the preceding MySQL example, except implemented in a MS Access database, we can show how to query and analyze the data using a visual tool. The following figure shows the contents of the two tables, USERS and COMMENTS.

(Continued)

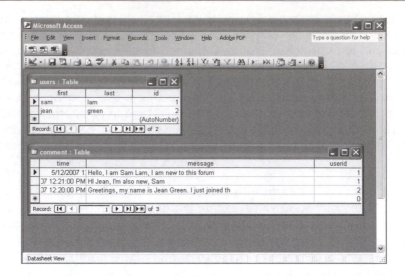

We have to set up the relationship between the ID field in the USER table and the USERID field in the COMMENTS table. Pull down the Tools menu and select Relationships ... . You should see a list of the two tables. Add both tables and close the panel. Then click on ID in the USER panel, and drag to the USERID in the COMMENTS panel. A line will now extend between them showing the relationship.

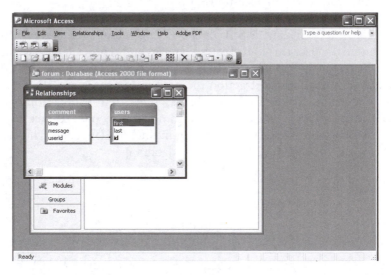

Then create the query, using the Create Query in Design View tool. Again add the USERS table and then the COMMENTS table and close the panel. Then select in order the USERS.FIRST, USERS.LAST, COMMENTS.TIME and COMMENTS.MESSAGE fields.

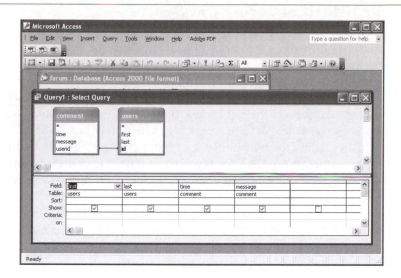

Then close the query box and select YES to save it. Double clicking the new Query icon, will then run the query and show the results.

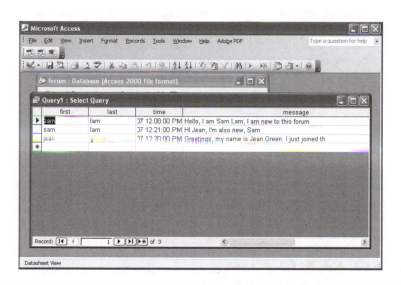

Researchers with knowledge of procedural and/or script programming can make use of application interfaces to the DBMS and make SQL operations directly from programs. For example, the **phpMyAdmin** application uses the application interface to **MySQL** built in to the PHP language.

Downloading the database

For the analysis of the data, the user will probably want to transfer them from the server to a local system. It is more convenient for sure, and in some cases it is not possible for an ordinary user to access the entire data store from the server. The data storage for the systems cannot be transferred directly from one computer to another; the data must first be dumped or exported. The export operation saves the data to a text file, which may be in one of several formats. Most typically the output file is a sequence of commands that can be applied to the database program to recreate the database. This is most useful if the database will be recreated on another computer. Alternatively, the data may sometimes be exported to an XML format, or perhaps to a comma-separated-variable (CSV) format; which may be convenient to import into a different kind of application, like a spreadsheet, or a textual analysis application. In any case, the resulting text files can be transferred between computers using standard network file transfer method such as FTP, or perhaps SCP (secure shell copy).

One of the benefits of the SQL language standard is that a dump into SQL from one database system can be used to recreate the data in a different database system from a different vendor. This is not 100 per cent accurate as there are small differences between the different applications' usage of SQL (despite the fact that it is a standard), but the differences are minor and can usually be managed with some editing. So a user could dump data from **MySQL** and load the data into **MS SQLServer** on their local system. **MS Access** and **FileMaker Pro** also have import functions to receive data from external sources; but since neither of them accepts SQL commands, the data will need to be exported from the database in CSV or perhaps XML form.

Geographic data files

Some data are most usefully displayed using maps. Public health data, census data and consumer product preferences, for example, often have a geographic component. In other words, the data of interest vary by region, and analysis of the data will tend to include representing the data on a map of some sort. Geographic data have their own specialized formats, which include the data of interest, say voter percentages, and a location on a map of where the information comes from, a city or county for example. Geographic Information Systems (GIS) usually use a paradigm of defining a geographic region using a "shape" which may be a point in the case of a city location, a set of line segments in the case of a road or a river, or a polygon in the case of a political boundary or physical structure. These shapes are stored in one or more files. The shapes have attributes which are the properties of interest to the researcher, and the attributes are stored in a simple database format and have a pointer to the associated shape, so that the GIS application can select an appropriate way to display the shape. In general, it is difficult to convert

GIS data into more general formats. Geographic data are best handled by dedicated GIS applications; we will describe a simple application in Chapter 11.

Application log files

Another type of data is generated automatically by server software. A variety of server applications keep logs and these are sometimes useful for research. For instance, web servers generally log each page request made to the server. A researcher may want to examine or summarize the contents of such logs. The two most common web server applications are **Apache**, which runs on Unix/Linux, Mac OS X and Windows, and **IIS** (Internet Information Server) which runs on Windows (NT and above). Apache is an open-source program and freely downloadable, IIS is integral to Windows, but not generally installed unless on Windows Server.

The Apache log is a text file, in which for each page request, a line contains by default the IP network address of the computer requesting the page, the date and time of the request, the request type and the page requested, the response code from the server, the number of characters sent, and the type of browser that made the request.

```
65.55.210.49 - - [19/Aug/2007:04:07:27 -0400] "GET/robots.txt
HTTP/1.0" 200 183 "-" "msnbot/1.0 (+ http://search.msn.com/ msnbot.htm)"
```

The logging can be configured with different options in Apache if desired. Generally, IP addresses are put in the log file because doing the reverse lookup from IP address to computer DNS name is time-consuming, and a busy web server will not be able to keep up with the requests. The response code is a numerical code indicating success (200), not found (404) and various other possibilities. In the above example, the browser is actually the MSN web crawler updating its search catalog.

If only a summary of web access is desired, there are programs such as **awstat** (awstats.sourceforge.net), **webalizer** (www.mrunix.net/webalizer) and **analog** (www.analog.cx) that can generate summaries with optional histogram and pie-chart graphics. These programs generally handle the conversion of IP addresses to DNS computer names.

If more fine-grained analysis of the log files is required, the log files can be parsed with your favorite text-processing application (your author (AES) favors the perl language for tasks like these). The fields should be separated, the date should be converted into a desired format, some special symbols may need to be unencoded, and then the output saved into a desired format, perhaps a table or a database.

Be aware that the IP address (or computer name) can be used to a limited extent to identify the user who made the web page request. Additionally, some URLs may contain extra parameters that might have sensitive data like passwords. If there are any applicable privacy concerns, they should be considered when publishing results from these data.

Accessing data sets online

Datasets may also originate from agencies such as the Census Bureau, the World Bank, the Department of Health and Human Services, or other research think-tank data banks for secondary research purposes. These data may be in the form of text files, or may be structured application data such as MS Excel data or many others.

There are a number of ways in which research is conducted through the collection of online data. In some instances, quantitative information may be available. In other cases, research may be on user habits derived through the analysis of user statistics. It's important to note, however, that this type of research is currently subject to debate regarding privacy laws as evidenced by the release of user data by America Online (AOL) and the subsequent backlash (e.g. Kirk, 2006). In other instances, web page content is analyzed for any number of purposes. Images, sounds, videos and text all represent types of data that could be useful for certain types of studies. In addition, many data sources are readily available online, making the internet a potential gold mine for quantitative analysis. One significant catch to culling online statistics, however, is finding sources. To that end, Genie Tyburski, in "Unearthing Statistical Data on the Internet: Effective Research Strategies," offers helpful hints and insights for online data searches (http://www.llrx.com/columns/stats.htm); http://web.worldbank.org/WBSITE/EXTERNAL/DATASTATISTICS/0,,menuPK:232599~pagePK:64133170~piPK:64133498~theSitePK:239419,00.html; or http://www.imf.org/external/data.htm.

Before discussing details of downloading and managing data found on the internet, there are a few questions that typically need to be asked about online data. There are obvious questions for a researcher to address, such as whether or not s/he is comfortable with the quality of the data for the purposes for which they will be used. But first and foremost is the question of whether or not data found on the internet should be treated as in public domain. Does the availability of information online imply fair use? What is often referenced in discussions on this topic is legality. The implication is that if the use of data is legal, then the use is acceptable. Outside of the ethical questions related to this topic, there are also copyright restrictions.

Though copyright regulations vary from country to country and can be a source of contention in international economic and political dialog, there are some general rules from which any researcher would benefit. On a basic level, Steven Imparl suggests that it is prudent to avoid any type of copyright infringement (2006: 3–52). In his *Internet Law: The Complete Guide*, he suggests that all forms of internet communication be treated as protected, which would include email, postings on mailing lists, interactive chats, web content, graphics, sounds, videos, communication by internet phone or video conferencing and e-book. He further advises users to "obtain written permission from the copyright owner for any material on the Internet that you wish to copy or use." Outside of obtaining written permission, which may not always be possible, it is good practice to give credit and reference for all information obtained on the internet.

Example
Accessing data from the International Monetary Fund

- Navigate to the IMF's data website (http://www.imf.org/external/data.htm).
- Navigate through the selections to your chosen region and to your choice of variables (the IMF site provides check boxes next to your variable options).
- After creating a report of your request data variables, you are provided with an option to download.
- You'll then see a screen that will be familiar to many users:

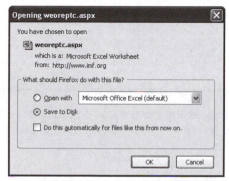

If you open the file, it will appear on your desktop as an Excel spreadsheet

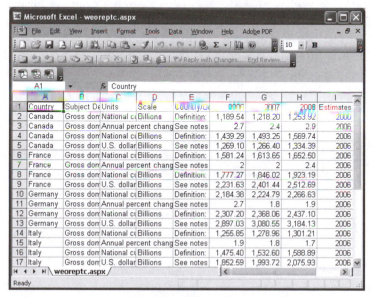

If you "save it to disk," the data will appear as a **Notes** file on your desktop. When you open it, you will see

(Continued)

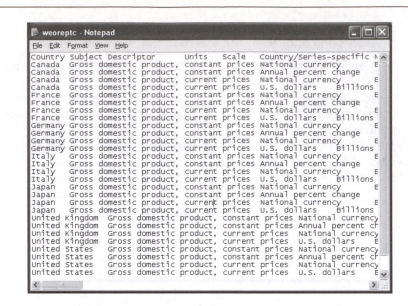

For most people, accessing the data as an Excel spreadsheet will be the most productive, as it's easily imported into a statistical application.

The types of analysis that lend themselves to downloading data include quantitative secondary analysis. Another researcher's data published online is a good example. In addition, academic think-tanks and organizations such as the US Federal Reserve and the World Bank often make their socio-economic data available for secondary analysis. Other research techniques might be narrative analysis, using blog data, or content analysis using blog and web site content. User statistics might also be useful in network analysis and employed in answering other types of behavioral questions involving people's online activities. All of these research opportunities require the researcher to download and manage data available on the web.

The following are issues to consider when downloading data and some suggestions about how to manage data for analysis.

Downloading

In the simplest case, the data will be made available via a web site, and the user can then just use a web browser to click on the dataset and download it. Not all sites are well organized, however, so it's possible that it will take a while for you to find the specific data you want to use. Sometimes a log-in ID and password will be required. In other cases the download will be from a password-protected or a public FTP site, and the user can download using a command line FTP program in a terminal, or perhaps using a graphical client like **WS_FTP**. In addition, many organizations maintaining large datasets may require the completion of an online form, providing some details about the researcher, as well as indicating which specific variables are being requested.

Large datasets are often in the form of compressed archives when made available for download. There are several possible formats, such as zip or gzip. Windows XP has a built-in expander for these data. Older versions of Windows may need a program like WinZip or P7zip. On the Macintosh, StuffIt Expander will extract data, or there are the Unix tools available in the command terminal, such as unzip or gunzip. Keep in mind that even if the file is compressed, it's much easier to download data on to a computer with high-speed internet access. Slow connections can have a tendency to terminate before a download is complete.

Before leaving a data site it is wise to double-check to make sure your data came with a codebook. Without a codebook your data are essentially worthless, as you are unable to interpret the numbers. Typically, a codebook is generated by the server. If a codebook doesn't come with the data, you may need to search the site or look for another data source.

Tips 'n Tricks

Downloading data

- Finding data on a site can be difficult. Not all sites are intuitive or well organized.
- Be prepared to complete online forms with personal information as well as the specifics of what you're requesting.
- Double-check data set size to make sure your host server won't limit your download.
- Be sure you receive a codebook with your data.
- Use a computer with a high-speed connection to make it easier to download and decrease the chance of terminating before completion.
- Open datasets in a spreadsheet first for cleaning data before analysis and for reformatting for a variety of statistical applications.

*Adapted from Neustadt, Robinson & Kestnbaum, 2002.

Data storage

Data storage is as much a research responsibility as it is a technical question. In some respects, the nature of the data is going to drive storage requirements. For example, medical data and medical related data have very strict mandated privacy and security requirements for storage. Typically, for example, the storage volume must not be available on any network. Other requirements may be that the data must be backed up and stored for a mandated length of time.

When data are stored on a computer, the owner must ensure that access permissions are appropriate for the degree of privacy required of the data. At a minimum, data should be in a password-protected account and not readable by other accounts. More stringent protection is provided by encryption of the data. Some of these points were discussed in Chapter 3.

Tips 'n Tricks

How to encrypt a file in Windows

(Users must be using Windows NT, Windows 2000, Windows XP, Windows Server 2003, and Windows Vista.)

You can encrypt files only on volumes that are formatted with the NTFS file system. To encrypt a file:

1. Click **Start**, point to **All Programs**, point to **Accessories** and then click **Windows Explorer**.
2. Locate the file that you want, right-click the file, and then click **Properties**.
3. On the **General** tab, click **Advanced**.
4. Under **Compress** or **Encrypt attributes**, select the **Encrypt contents to secure data** check box, and then click **OK**.
5. If the file is located in an unencrypted folder, you receive an Encryption Warning dialog box. Use one of the following steps:

   - If you want to encrypt only the file, click **Encrypt the file only**, and then click **OK**.
   - If you want to encrypt the file and the folder in which it is located, click **Encrypt the file and the parent folder**, and then click **OK**.

Another user attempting to open an encrypted file cannot do so. For example, if another user attempts to open an encrypted Microsoft Word document, that user receives a message similar to:

Word cannot open the document: *username* does not have access privileges (*drive*:*filename*.doc)

If another user attempts to copy or move an encrypted document to another location on the hard disk, the following message appears:

Error Copying File or Folder

Cannot copy *filename*: Access is denied.

Make sure the disk is not full or write-protected and that the file is not currently in use.

If, however, a research endeavor involves more than one researcher, after a file has been encrypted it is possible to add users, granting permission to particular individuals to read encrypted files.

* From Microsoft Corporation's support web site: http://support.microsoft. com/kb/307877 accessed on 23 August 2007.

On a multi-user machine or networked machine, make sure that file permissions are set to prevent unauthorized user access, preventing others from reading or copying files.

Tips 'n Tricks

How to restrict access to a file or folder in Windows

The setting of file or folder access permissions in Windows depends on whether the computer is on a Windows Domain, or on a Windows Workgroup, or completely off the network. It also depends on whether the disk volume is formatted with NTFS or the FAT format. Generally in enterprises, the computer will be part of a domain, and the disks will be formatted with NTFS. A computer at home will probably not be on a domain. Also, only computers with Windows NT and later, can be part of a domain.

If not on a domain, only folder permissions may be set, not individual files. The procedure is:

1. In Windows Explorer, right-click on the folder, and select **Properties**.
2. Select the **Sharing** tab.
3. Click on the "**Make the folder private**" check box to set it.
4. Click **Ok** or **Apply**. If you do not have a password set for your account, there will be no value in this because anyone can log in as you, so the computer will ask you if you want to set a password at this time.

If on a domain, and if the volume is formatted with NTFS, then the access permissions are much more granular (and complicated). You can set the permissions on a folder or a single file.

1. In Windows Explorer, right-click on the folder, and select **Properties**.
2. Select the **Security** tab.

(Continued)

3. Two panels will appear, the top one with a list of **Users** and **Groups**, and the bottom one, with a list of **Permissions** to allow or deny.
4. Any user not in the list of users will have no access permissions to the file or folder. But be aware that a user may be part of one of the listed groups. You can select any user or group in the list, and click **Remove**. Generally, however, you do not want to remove the **Administrators** group and the **SYSTEM** group.
5a. To add more users to the list if desired, click on **Add.** A new panel **"Select Users, Computers or Groups"** will appear. You can change the location, but let us assume that the default location, which is your current domain, is **OK.**
5b. If you know the exact domain ID of the user, type that into the **"Object Names to Select"** text box. If not, enter a partial name, and click on **"Check Names"**.
5c. Select the correct name, and click **OK.**
6. Check or uncheck the appropriate permissions to enable the degree of access you want.

Research data are often unique and therefore in practical terms priceless. Making backups of datasets is the best protection against accidental loss. Computers break down and users make mistakes, so a duplicate copy of the data is an absolute necessity. Even better, the backup copy should be stored somewhere widely separated from the original, in case some disaster occurs, such as a flood or a fire. Backups can be simply copies of files on to a removable disk drive, which then needs to be moved to a safe place. Or the files can be duplicated to another computer in a different location. Or, lastly, the data can be backed up to data tape using a backup application. Tapes have the advantage that they are easier to remove from a system and transport. On the other hand, tape backup systems tend to be somewhat expensive.

In this chapter we've provided you with a general overview regarding accessing data on the web. We hope that some of the tips about how to download data, and things like encrypting and restricting access to data will aid you in your research. The following chapter will focus on using the data once you have them.

9 ANALYZING THE DATA

There is no department of inquiry in which it is not just as easy to miss the truth as to find it, even when the materials from which truth is to be drawn are actually present to our senses.

Harriet Martineau

Chapter summary

- Selecting qualitative research software
- Working with HyperResearch & NVivo
- Working with quantitative research tools

So you've designed and developed your study, recruited participants, conducted the research, and have begun to organize the subsequent mounds of data. Now what? Obviously, we conduct research because we believe we'll validate our suspicions about some phenomenon or arrive at a new understanding about something. This leads us to the wonderful world of analysis.

There are a number of ways in which we can conduct analysis. Some of us still use the tried and true paper and pencil methods, and maybe a calculator, to quantify basic univariate statistical measures, while others organize note cards and slips of paper that indicate ideas that emerged from interviews. Today, however, the majority of us are more likely to start up our computer and use some type of analytical tool designed for our particular method of analysis. As a qualitative researcher, we might use HyperResearch to code and organize our data. As a quantitative researcher, we might turn to SPSS or the basic statistical functions in Microsoft's Excel. If we happen to be a fan of triangulation, a research approach that involves the use of different research methods as a means of improving research validity, we might even be using a combination of the two.

Whatever our research endeavor, it will undoubtedly involve some type of analysis. Even if we're an ethnographer who believes strongly that it is not our place, as researchers, to interpret or analyze a participant's words, but rather to give voice to his or her story, we have to decide which stories we'll include and how we'll present that data – which is, arguably, a kind of analysis.

Today, there are a number of software programs designed to aid the researcher in data management and the analysis of data. The following pages will offer some general guidelines and tips for selecting software and provide some general information for performing analysis. The first section will discuss qualitative analysis and offer some guidance regarding the selection of qualitative software packages. The later section will provide some general advice for working with quantitative analytical tools. As with other chapters, there are a number of resources identified throughout the chapter for a more complete coverage of specific topics.

Qualitative analysis

As noted by Anselm Strauss and Juliet Corbin, "by the term qualitative research we mean any kind of research that produces findings not arrived at by means of statistical procedures or other means of quantification" (1990: 17). To be clear, qualitative research takes on various forms, with some focused on as little analysis as possible and others using various types of schema to develop theories and findings. For example, in *Rachel and Her Children: Homeless Families in America*, Jonathan Kozol asks: "Why are so many people homeless in our nation? What has driven them to the streets? What hope have they to reconstruct their former lives? The answer will be told in their own words" (1988: 3). Strauss and Corbin elaborate on this diversity, noting that, "Some of the different types of qualitative research are: grounded theory, ethnography, the phenomenological approach, life history and conversational analysis" (1990: 21). Each type will have its own analytical needs.

Christopher Hahn (2008) notes that although qualitative researchers are diverse in their use of various research methods and assumptions, they also share common challenges. They generate a great deal of data, the management of that data is integral to the success of a study, and the analysis of the data requires tools that enable a researcher to focus on the research questions at the heart of the study.

As a rule, qualitative research has three major components: data, some procedure for analyzing the data, and some kind of output of the findings (Lewins & Silver, 2007). The data can be in many forms. Today, data can be in the form of text, video or audio files. In all cases these could be from an interview, a focus group, an observational note or an observation of some type of behavior. The procedure is typically some form of coding, structured or unstructured, by which data are identified in some meaningful way to aid in the analysis. Output can vary just as widely as a collection of video edits designed to highlight a phenomenon, or interspersed in a presentation or a written report or paper conveying the research findings.

Choosing qualitative software

There are a number of good applications on the market, and all of them have strengths and weaknesses. As you discern which is right for you, keep in mind that the way a particular program functions, technologically, may have an impact on study findings. As pointed out by Christine Barry, some feel that different packages transform the data in different ways and that this in turn encourages different ways of thinking about data and theory (1998. paragraph 3.2. http://www.socresonline.org.uk/socresonline/3/3/4.html). As the technology of qualitative applications continues to evolve, the challenge for a researcher is to do the necessary homework to determine which application is the best for his or her particular purposes. To that end, Weitzman and Miles (1995) offer four key questions:

1. What kind of computer user am I?
2. Am I choosing for one project or the next few years?
3. What kind of project(s) and database(s) will I be working on?
4. What kind of analysis am I planning to do?

In addition to these questions, we suggest you also consider what type of user support is accessible to you, in conjunction with the question of your own computer skills. Some institutions have strong support organizations with professionals who are equipped to assist in troubleshooting software problems. There may be technical staff, or graduate assistants in a university environment, with strong computer backgrounds, who have the ability and time to assist with troubleshooting. If you are working independently, for example as a consultant with a home office, consider whether or not you have access to individuals who could help if needed. The essential point is that if the answer to question one is that you are "a low-level user," then using a sophisticated application is likely to cause frustration and require assistance of some kind. Failing to assess the need for assistance can be a costly mistake in terms of time, money and frustration level, if assistance is required and not readily available. This point also implies that you take into account the user-friendliness of any application under consideration.

Popular Qualitative Software

HyperResearch http://www.researchware.com
NVivo http://www.qsrinternational.com/products_nvivo.aspx
Atlas/ti http://www.atlasti.com
Ethnograph http://www.qualisresearch.com
MAXQDA http://www.maxqda.com

Assessing applications and their capabilities can be done by searching online. Most applications are represented in web pages describing the basics of the application, core features, and who might benefit from using it. Many provide tutorials within the application and also offer them online. For example, one popular qualitative application, NVivo 7, available through QSR International, provides an online tutorial (http://www.qsrinternational.com/support_tutorials.aspx) which makes it possible to get a sense of the application before making a purchase. In addition, several applications, such as HyperResearch available through ResearchWare (http://www.research ware.com/hr/downloads.html), provide a free downloadable version of their application with a limited-use restriction, enabling a researcher to use some of the features of the product before investing in a license.

Tips 'n Tricks

Choosing a Qualitative Analysis Application

As you evaluate qualitative analysis applications, some questions to keep in mind include:

- What type of data do you need to analyze? Are these text? Are they in some kind of database or simply text files? In what form is the text? Can you save files as text only?
- How many cases will you have? And will you need to differentiate the cases? (In most situations, you will.)
- What kind of analysis are you anticipating? Will your work be exploratory, in that you'll be developing many kinds of codes in a grounded theory approach to analysis?
- How will you want your coding to be organized? Will you want/need your codes quantified for reporting purposes?
- Do you have any cost constraints/limitations that serve as a driver for your purchase? For example, will you need multiple licenses for staff or a single user? Does the company provide a multi-user license at a discount? Or will you pay the same per license, regardless of the number purchased?
- Among other support related questions, does the vendor provide any kind of workshops or trainings? Are they online, hosted in your local area, or do you need to travel to them?

Once you've made your selection, you'll need to begin working with the data to be analyzed. In most cases, data should be saved as a text only file (.txt) or as a rich text file (.rtf). Before opening a qualitative application, determine which type of format is necessary for your data. Save all data files (i.e. interviews, focus group discussions, etc.) in the proper format, adding any additional required symbols. Once the data are ready for use, open the application and import the data as instructed for coding. The following examples will give you a sense of how coding works in two popular software packages, HyperResearch and NVivo.

HyperResearch

A basic version of HyperResearch is available for download from the ResearchWare web site (www.researchware.com). The free trial version is a good way to evaluate the program before purchasing it. It is a fully functioning application, but limits the master code list to 75 codes, the study to seven cases, and each case to 50 code instances. These limitations don't present a problem for testing the application, but would become a constraint for a large study. The point here is not to try and be clever by using the free download as your analytical application, because you'll eventually run into problems.

The following image shows the basic structure for doing analysis in HyperResearch. On the right is an interview file. It is a text file and is imported into the program as a text file. On the left is a different window, identifying the contents of the study. Note that there are several codes such as "places family needs above self" identified from interview one. In this way, all of the codes created for each interview are identified in the "study" window and are easily managed and utilized for generating theory and testing hypotheses.

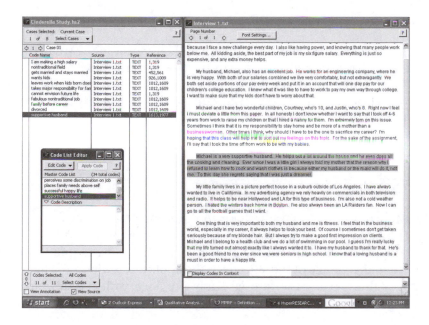

*Examples are drawn from the Cinderella Study available as a tutorial with the HyperResearch software package.

In the lower left hand corner there is a code list editor that lists all of the codes created in the study. To code the interview, see box below.

Example
Coding in HyperResearch

1. Select (highlight) a block of text in the interview by scrolling over it with your mouse, ... for example
   Michael is a very supportive husband. He helps out a lot around the house and he even does all the cooking and cleaning. Ever since I was a little girl I always told my mother that the reason why I refused to learn how to cook and wash clothes is because either my husband or the maid will do it, not me. To this day she regrets saying that I was just a dreamer.
2. Either select a code in the **Code Editor**, or select the option for **new code** from the Edit Code drop-down menu. For example, you might create a code entitled "supportive husband."
3. After the code appears in your list, double-click on it with the text in the interview still highlighted. Your new code will be associated with the highlighted text.

The text code with the text identifiers will then appear in the study window. In this way, that text is identified with that particular code. The text can be coded again either in its entirety or as a sub-section. The code can also be edited or "clustered" or "nested" with other codes as a theory begins to take shape from working with the data.

NVivo

NVivo functions in a similar fashion to other qualitative software applications. It builds its own internal database as data are imported. All of the data for a study go into one file called a project. In the following example, projects are listed in the middle of the left side of the application window. The project listed is **Volunteering**, the tutorial study provided with the downloadable demonstration version of NVivo. A double-click on Volunteering opens the study.

As a database, the application organizes all of your source files into a directory. To review the directory and access a particular source file, all the user needs to do is select **Sources** in the lower left side menu. Selecting **Sources** while in the Volunteer field yields the following listing.

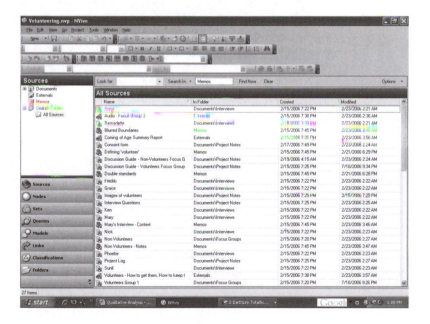

Example
Coding Data in NVivo

1. Select (highlight) the data you want to code. (In the example, the text is "Sometimes it's a thankless task.")
2. Right-click on the text. When the menu appears, select **Code** and **Code Selection at New Node**. This will allow you to create a new code.
3. In the naming menu, click on **Selection** in the upper right corner.
4. On the left, select **Tree Nodes**. On the right side will be a list of tree nodes. Let's say that we believe that we've discovered a new code we want to call "thankless" and it fits well within the tree nodes of **experiences of volunteer** and **negative**. To create this new code, highlight **negative** and click the **OK** button.
5. In the blank for **Name**, we would type **thankless**. It's a good practice to type a few notes regarding details as to why the code was selected and any referential details.
6. When finished naming the code and typing notes, select **OK**. In the upper window of tree nodes, **thankless** should appear in the listing under **negative**. If you double-click on **thankless** in the tree node listing, the text highlighted to create the code should be listed.

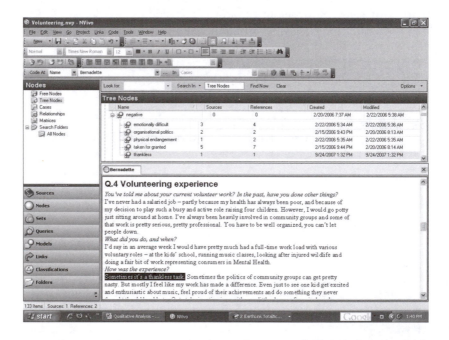

In the preceding examples, we've offered basics for demonstrating some of the intuitiveness of working with qualitative analytical applications. The examples are only a teaser, to help the user understand qualitative applications. For those in need of a more sophisticated, in-depth treatment of the topic, we recommend Lewins and Silver's *Using Software in Qualitative Research: A Step-by-Step Guide* (2007). Although the tutorials are focused on three applications (Atlas.ti 5, MAXqda 2 and NVivo 7), the detail and organization of the text are very user-friendly, and the lessons gleaned from the opening chapters are applicable across any of the qualitative applications. The power of these applications, however, is demonstrated more fully by working with the theoretical tools. Using coding schemes to build relationships and visualize patterns in the data is where analysis leads to the generation of new concepts, theories and understandings of a research topic.

Researchers looking for more detailed technical information, more extensive assistance in selecting an application, or more specific guidance in how to use a qualitative research application are encouraged to access other resources such as:

> Ann Lewins and Christina Silver (2007) *Using Software in Qualitative Research: A Step-by-Step Guide.* London: Sage Publications.
> Eben A. Weitzman and Matthew B. Miles (1995) *Computer Programs for Qualitative Data Analysis*, Thousand Oaks, CA: Sage Publications.
> http://caqdas.soc.surrey.ac.uk
> http://www.quarc.de/body_overview.html

There is a great deal of information, together with publicly available articles on selecting and working with qualitative software, available on the internet. Though Weitzman and Miles is a dated reference (1995), with limited utility regarding the actual software packages, it still contains a great deal of useful information in the early chapters. Once you have a sense of the types of packages you're interested in, most will have websites with information about their current functionality and often provide links for downloading a trial version. It is not recommended, however, that you begin analysis with a trial version, as most have limited functionality, are only accessible for a particular period of time, and/or lack the ability to save your work.

Quantitative analysis

Quantitative analysis is, by definition, about numbers. The object of quantitative analysis is usually to chart the data, or to derive some generalization or statistic from them such as means, medians or some other trends. If we're looking for basic univariate statistical measures, where only one dimension of a given population is being considered at a time, then we might be interested in a mean, a median or a variance. If we're considering bivariate or multivariate statistics, we might be employing analytical techniques such as regression analysis or forecasting.

This chapter is designed for the statistical novice and is not meant to be a support in conducting statistical analysis specifically. Rather, it is our intention to provide you with some assistance in working with the data to do the analysis. It has been our experience that the majority of researchers are quite comfortable with using their favorite statistical application. But when it comes to working with raw data, they often discover they lack the necessary information and skill to transfer their data into their favorite statistical package.

On one occasion, we were working with a group of nurses. They had received a grant from the NIH to conduct a particular type of research, and the grant came with access to a wealth of federal data. What they weren't told was that the data would arrive on outdated reel-to-reel tapes in the outdated format of an outdated software package. They arrived on our doorstep with a very large, very heavy, box of tapes. Once we were able to get the data off of the tapes and into Excel files, they cleaned the data and transferred it into a statistical package. While we don't offer any advice on how to deal with outdated technology, the following pages will focus on cleaning and working with data.

The focus of this chapter is to enable you to work with any dataset that comes in Excel or can be transferred by you into Excel. We selected Excel because it is widely available and most users are familiar with its general functionality. It is our hope that this brief section will coach you through the preparation of datasets for analysis.

The data

Original quantitative data may come from any number of sources and in many possible formats. The data could be typed in by hand or downloaded from a web or FTP site, or they may be the output of some application run locally. They may be in a text file, or a spreadsheet or some other application-specific file format.

Text files are called unstructured because they are (usually) just a continuous stream of characters. Even though the data on each line of the text file may be arranged in a certain way, there is nothing about the file format that enforces this arrangement. So when data from a text file are read by an application, there must be some definition of how the application understands the data on each line. Usually this comes down to knowing what separates one variable from the next. The most common separators are "white" space (blanks, tabs and carriage returns) or punctuation marks such as commas or colons. There may be no separator; the variables are defined by their column position on a line. This last format was much more common in the punch-card era; there is less need to conserve file space these days, but the format can still be found.

Spreadsheets offer the advantage that the file format itself knows what separates one variable from another, every variable is a single cell, at the intersection of one row and one column of the spreadsheet. However, text format files do still have some advantages; particularly on Linux/Unix systems, or in the Unix mode of Mac OS X. Unix and Linux come with dozens of program and scripting languages that are specifically designed for manipulating text files, and the degree of processing that is possible with these tools is nearly infinite. On Windows it is more difficult, though it is possible to install some of these programs. On Windows text file manipulation is more often done with packaged software, SAS being one example.

If the researcher is comfortable with text files and scripting, they may choose to stay in that format; but in all likelihood most researchers will convert their data into a spreadsheet at a fairly early stage. Spreadsheet applications are very useful all-in-one packages for manipulating data and performing calculations on the data. Many people believe that the spreadsheet is one of the main reasons that use of personal computers grew so rapidly in the 1980s.

Example
Importing a text file into Excel

Spreadsheets can import text file in certain formats. We show an example with comma-separated variables (CSV). The input file, called "input-data.txt", looks as follows:

1, 10, 3030
2, 12, 5510
3, 11, 6800
4, 9, 5403
5, 8, 4930

We start MS Excel (Mac OS X version in this example), and open the file:

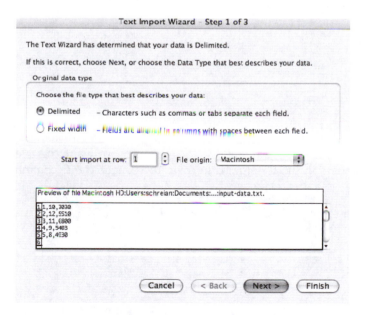

The defaults are OK, click **Next**:

(Continued)

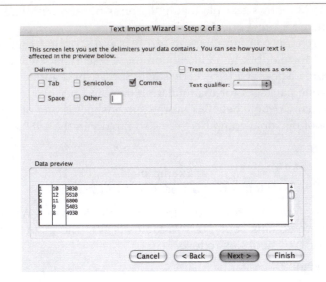

Choose the **Comma** check box and click **Finish**. The data will be inserted into your spreadsheet. Save the file as an Excel spreadsheet.

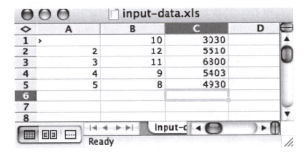

A spreadsheet program like Excel or Calc, allows for analysis of the enclosed data with formulas. If, for example, we want the average of the numbers in the C columns in rows 1-4, select the C column.

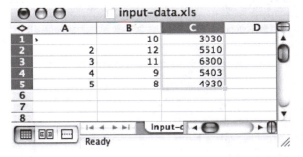

Then choose the "**Average**" function from the toolbar, and it will place the computed average at the below the selection into cell C:6.

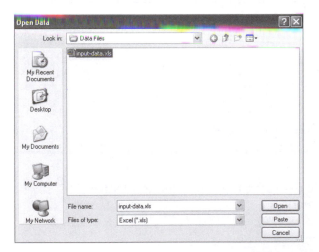

The handy thing here is that C:6 contains a formula, not just a number, so if the contents of C:3 are changed, then the formula will update the result in C:6 automatically. This is why business users find spreadsheets so useful for exploratory data analysis.

Excel and Calc have fairly good selection of tools and formulas, but for more sophisticated analysis many researchers will want to import their data into programs such as SPSS, SAS, Stata or perhaps Matlab or IDL. Here we show how to import an Excel (xls) spreadsheet into SPSS and then SAS.

Example
Importing an Excel spreadsheet into SPSS

The SPSS application imports spreadsheets in a straightforward way. Start up SPSS, with a new empty dataset. Then choose from the **File** menu, **Open->Data....** In the file browser dialog navigate to the right folder, and set the **Files of Type** to "Excel (ˆ.xls)" or "All Files (ˆ.ˆ)". Double-click on your spreadsheet file, or select it and click the **Open** button.

(Continued)

One more dialog will come up to help you select data ranges. In our case we will use all the data, and also uncheck the **Read variable** names from first the row of the data box, because our input file does not use that.

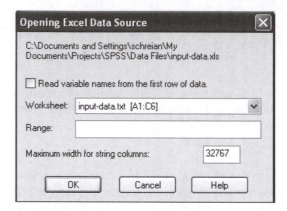

SPSS will open a document viewer to show you the log file of the command just executed, and will place the data into the data sheet as shown here.

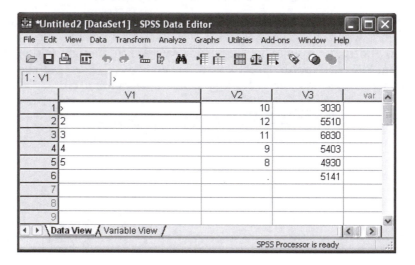

You should then save the datasheet as a native SPSS .sav file, and then continue working.

Example
Importing an Excel spreadsheet into SAS

SAS is a somewhat more daunting application than SPSS, but the importation of data is not difficult. Start SAS with an new empty datasheet. From the **File** menu, choose **Import Data...** . An import wizard will come up, and Excel is the default input format, so we can stick with that. At this point one could also import directly from text files and various other formats.

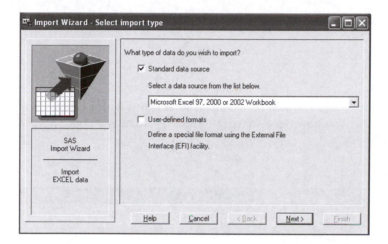

Click **Next**, and a **Connect to MS Excel** dialog will pop up. Browse to the folder containing your input file and select it. Then click **OK**.

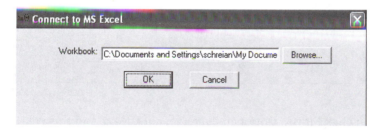

It then pops up a dialog asking which table you want to import, and in this case the default is fine.

(Continued)

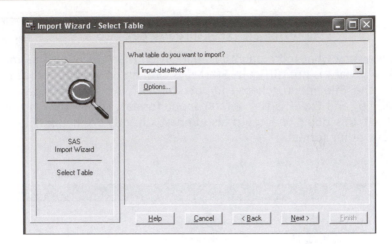

Click **Next** and you will be asked to select into which Library to import the data. You have to also assign a name to the Member; here we will use "input".

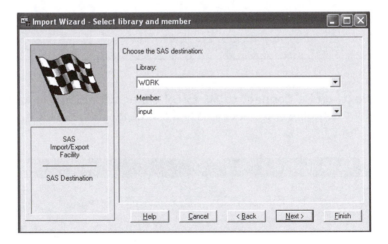

You can click **Finish**. Optionally you can click **Next** and this will let you save the SAS program that reads the input file; but we skip that step. Finally the input dataset gets placed in your library; and you can select that to show and work with the data.

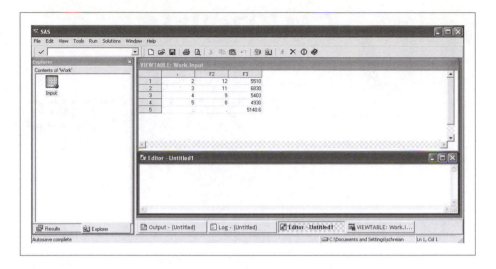

Many applications will read Excel (.xls) spreadsheets directly, but for some cases of data importation it will be useful to use a program like Stat/Transfer that can translate data between many formats commonly used for statistical software. Information about Stat/Transfer can be found at http://www.stattransfer.com.

To use applications both for qualitative and quantitative analysis well can take some practice. Importing the data is only the first step. Spreadsheet applications such as Microsoft Excel, OpenOffice Calc, and Apple iWorks Numbers are the easiest but are somewhat limited. SPSS is also fairly easy to use but favors Windows. SAS is a large program that does many things in addition to data anlysis. It has a fairly steep learning curve but is ultimately very powerful. Other applications such as Stata, Matlab and IDL require a mindset of writing programs, but can therefore be very flexible and powerful. Most applications have a tutorial and many often publish guide books.

Though brief, we hope the outline in the preceding pages was of assistance if you are beginning your analysis. While we questioned the utility of such a limited presentation of analytical tools, we also recognize that for those just getting started, the types of issues we've raised and the basic steps we've presented may just be the ticket for getting you launched on your analysis.

10 EMERGING RESEARCH OPPORTUNITIES

Chapter summary

- Social network analysis offers new opportunities for visualizing relationships.
- Virtual worlds offer new opportunities for observing human behavior.
- Online gaming can provide rich data by engaging participants in simulations.

There are some technologies and online research techniques that are not prevalent, but demonstrate the ways in which online research is evolving and the ways in which technologies can provide new opportunities. The following examples of social network analysis, observation in virtual worlds and gaming all represent ways in which online research is maturing and providing new opportunities for researchers. The purpose of this chapter is to provide you with a general overview, as opposed to providing you with "how to" instructions. While the information offered is limited, we have attempted to provide sufficient information to enable those interested in venturing further to acquire a vision of how to pursue these emerging opportunities and links.

Social network analysis

A somewhat different type of data is used to analyze social networks. The goal of social network analysis is to determine the connectedness and clustering, among other properties, of individuals in a community. "Social network analysis seeks to describe networks of relations as fully as possible, tease out the prominent patterns in such networks, trace the flow of information (and other resources) through them, and discover what effects these relations and networks have on people and organizations" (Garton, Haythornthwait & Wellman, 1999: 76). The data may take many forms, but require some way to show that one item is, or is not, connected to another; sometimes this takes the form of a matrix. The analyst considers all of the connections and attempts to group and arrange them in meaningful ways. Content, direction and strength are the ways in which relationships are described.

Data for analysis are gathered by a variety of methods. Questionnaires, interviews, diaries, user log files, observations and computer monitoring are all used to acquire data. As Garton et al. note, a participant might be asked about the frequency of communication and also to specify the medium of interaction (1999: 90).

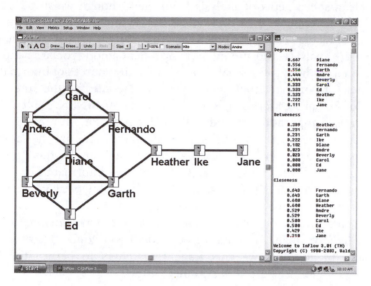

*The preceding image is from http://www.orgnet.com/sna.html, accessed on 14 September 2007.

The image above is a network analysis demonstrating the interconnectedness of a number of individuals, highlighting their particular relationships.

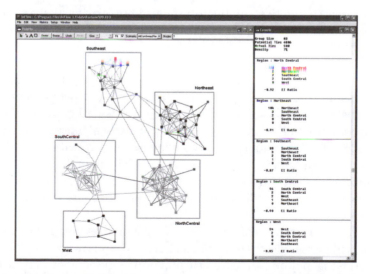

*The preceding image is from http://www.orgnet.com/inflow3.html, accessed on 14 September 2007.

To facilitate management of a study, including the development of data collection instruments, there are applications such as Network Genie (secure.network genie.com). As this type of research continues to grow, many more applications will emerge to support research efforts.

To be clear, social network analysis is not new, though we suspect few are familiar with it. As an analytical practice, at one time its needs exceeded the technology available. Today the technology has caught up with the need, and social network analysis is becoming more prevalent among social scientists and organizational studies professionals. There are many sources of information on the internet for software information such as the site for the International Network for Social Network Analysis (www.insna.org/ INSNA/soft_inf.html). Commonly used applications include UCINET, Krackplot, Multinet, NEGOPY, Gradap, FatCat, InFlow and Linkalign. Not all applications are the same, however. Some, such as InFlow, are designed for business use. Others are totally unrelated to "social" networks, and apply more to bioinformatics or computer network analysis. A general rule of thumb for researching network analysis and the various tools available is to read through some specifies about a given application and take a quick look at a data/analysis sample. The *Handbook of Online Research Methods* (Blank, Fielding & Lee, 2008) is a good source of general information. In addition, we encourage researchers to peruse the journal *Connections* (www. insna.org/indexConnect.html).

Observing behavior and virtual worlds

A type of research practiced on the internet is known as participant observation. There are many environments where this type of research is possible. The most basic type of observation can be performed in any number of communicative environments such as on a listserv discussion list or a chat room. Game rooms (e.g. http://www. mpogd.com/), where people interact in the context of some kind of gaming activity, are also fairly easy to access and can provide substantive observational data. There are also other kinds of interactive environments that lend themselves to participant observation such as Second Life (http://secondlife.com/), an online society within a 3D world, where users can explore, build, socialize and participate in their own economy (pacec-sped.org/pf6007.htm, accessed on 8 March 2007). Just about any place on the internet where individuals interact provides an environment for observing behavior.

Online virtual environments range from very simple text-based environments that originated over modem-based bulletin board systems, to some of the current virtual worlds that rely on 3-dimensional graphical representation and have much in common with computer video games. The basic systems are called MUDs

*http://secondlife.com

(Multi-user Dungeons) and were either for the purpose of hosting role-playing games (RPG) similar to Dungeons and Dragons, or on occasion used for distance learning. MOOs (Multi-user Object Oriented) are a variation on MUDs, allowing the user to extend the environment with programs. The current systems are known as MMORPGs (Massive multi-player online RPG), and include such video game experiences as World of Warcraft, and Second Life, which is not really a game with a goal, but closer to the concept of an online environment.

To evaluate these communal environments typically involves observing behavior much like sitting on the street corner and watching people interact. The obvious difference is that on a street corner anyone who wants to can be aware of your presence. Online, an observer can be present without anyone knowing that they are being observed. This type of observation online is referred to as lurking, and is often noted in pejorative terms. Lurking, most typically referring to some form of watching while concealed, is used on the internet to refer to those members of groups who read messages without contributing to a discussion (Sharf, 1999: 249). Some feel lurking is a violation of another person's rights and privacy in that they are being watched without their knowledge, and ought to be given the choice of whether or not they want to be subject to someone's voyeuristic electronic urges. Others, however, feel that the term lurking is over-used and may reflect something more like a non-participant or *observer* (from http://www.bc.edu/bc_org/avp/law/st_org/ iptf/commentary/content/1999060506.html, accessed on 24 January 2007). We refer you to both the online commentary as well as elsewhere in this book for a more extensive discussion of lurking.

The challenge for researchers is to determine whether or not their form of research necessitates participant-observation. If yes, then it is necessary to determine if acknowledgement of online observation is necessary and warranted. As noted by Henderson, ethically a researcher probably needs to inform research participants that they are being observed (2007: 379). However, it's also important to consider whether or not the knowledge of observation will impact findings. For a more substantive discussion of using the internet for ethnographic research, consider the work of Christine Hine, *Virtual Ethnography* (2000), and Andreas Wittel (2000).

In addition to determining when and if to reveal the researcher's presence in an online environment, it's also important to consider what types of social phenomena are appropriate for analysis in virtual environments, where people role-play, emboldened by the social distance and perceived anonymity of the online environment, and create representative likenesses of themselves. We can probably all agree that the online environment represents something, but just what it represents still needs to be determined.

Gaming as research

There are a number of ways in which online gaming can be used for research. In some instances games are the subject of research, with researchers studying the content with concerns about issues such as race, gender and violence. For example, Dave Grossman has researched extensively on the topic of violence in games (Grossman, 1996; Grossman & Degaetano, 1999). In other instances, researchers are interested in evaluating social interactions and community in gaming environments. Education professionals research gaming to understand the ways in which we learn from the engagement and the interaction, acquiring team-building skills, certain social skills, self-confidence, and so forth (see Prensky, 2006).

A unique area of research, however, involves a simulation which is, itself, a part of the research instrument. Most simulation research, to date, has focused on educational simulations. Data collection has been oriented around improving the efficacy of education and training models (Gibson, Aldrich & Prensky, 2007). However, other disciplines are beginning to see ways in which gaming data can be useful. For instance, a doctoral researcher in finance who is now a faculty member at the University of Maryland, Myeong-Gu Seo, used an internet-based stock investment simulation combined with an experience sampling method to examine the dynamics of affective experience and its effects on decision making in a real-life setting (Seo & Barrett, 2007). The simulation technique enabled him to isolate individual-level effects of affective experience from potential group-level, organizational-level, and institutional-level factors that could have impacted decision-making outcomes.

Sample from a Gaming Exercise

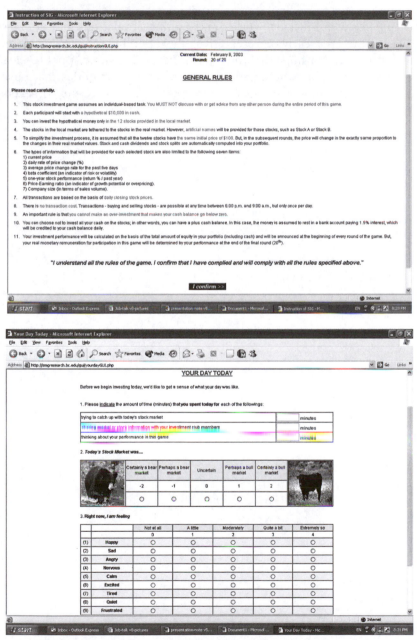

Source: personal archives of Myeong-Gu Seo.

While this type of project can require a significant amount of up-front programming, it represents a formidable method for data acquisition. As the world becomes more acclimated to interactive technologies, this type of research, which can be both fun and educational for participants, will certainly increase.

As noted, the preceding research techniques of social network analysis, observing behavior in virtual worlds, and gaming simulations may not be standard today, but are clearly representative of what online research will look like in the future. It is our hope that these pages have whet some appetites, leading some of you to explore these and other research opportunities that push the boundaries of our understanding of online research in the twenty-first century.

11 PRESENTING YOUR RESULTS

Chapter summary

- Charts and tables add to a document
- Charts can come from tabular data or other forms. There are many choices of applications to draw either type
- Geographic map data can be useful in some instances
- Consider whether others can read the file format you create

After all the data are collected and analyzed, finally we come to the subject of presenting the results – whether in a paper or report, or at an audience presentation, or on a web site. One key to the effective presentation of data is the inclusion of tables and figures. This chapter will discuss how to plot the data in the tables, and also how to plot other types of data that do not fit into a table format. And then we'll show how to incorporate these data tables and graphs into documents.

We will discuss some specific software applications, as we have to some extent in earlier chapters. We will try to cover the best known applications and offer an alternative or two; and also give examples on Windows, Mac OS X and Linux. The subject of software applications is a difficult one to cover concisely in a book. Because there is such a large variety of applications for any type of purpose, it is not possible to cover more than a subset of them in any detail. Moreover, software is frequently updated, and detailed information is usually current for only two to three years. We will endeavor to list the version of any application we mention, which is usually the current one at the time of writing. Much more detail is almost always available in documentation and tutorials, either at the vendor web site for commercial software, or the source site for open-source software. Excellent third-party tutorials can also frequently be found on the World Wide Web.

Microsoft, of course, dominates the desktop document creation industry. **Microsoft Office** is ubiquitous on Windows systems, and very common on Mac OS systems as well, but by choice they have ignored the Unix/Linux environment. There are, however, alternatives to Microsoft Office for all the platforms we are considering, one of the most significant of which is the **OpenOffice** suite. Apple also provides a cost-added feature for Mac OSX, **iWork**, which includes the **Keynote** for presentations and **Pages** for word processing. A further option is to use **Google Docs** to manage documents. This service provides presentation, spreadsheet and document services. Documents will be stored on the Google servers and a Google mail account is required.

At the time of writing, **Microsoft Office 2007** for Windows has just been released, but is only beginning to appear on computers so we will describe **Office 2003**. The current version of Microsoft Office for Mac OSX is **Office 2004**. The current version of OpenOffice is 2.4.

Creating graphics

Tables, charts

Perhaps the easiest way to chart numerical data is with a spreadsheet program like **Microsoft Excel** or **OpenOffice Calc**. Loading the data into a spreadsheet was covered previously; here we will demonstrate how to graph some existing data.

Example
Creating a Chart in Excel for Mac

The data are entered as one or more columns in the spreadsheet. To plot the data, select one or more columns, then select the Chart Wizard from the toolbar.

From this select the type of chart; choices are histogram, line chart, dot chart and pie charts, each in two or three dimensions.

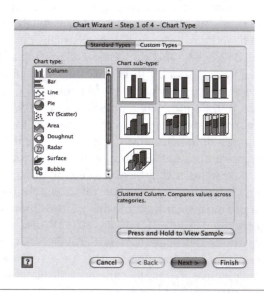

In most cases, you select bar chart (histogram), line plot or scatter plot. Continuing with the wizard, you can specify the plot title and axis labels.

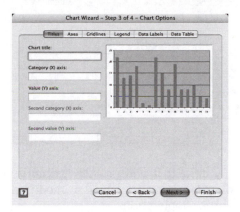

And finally, you can choose whether to place the resulting chart in the current worksheet, or create a new worksheet.

Example
Creating a chart with OpenOffice Calc

OpenOffice Calc is very similar to **Excel**. Enter data in rows and columns, select one or more rows and columns, and click on Insert Chart, then click the worksheet again (this step is different from Excel).

The chart wizard will open, and take you through some steps. Select the chart type:

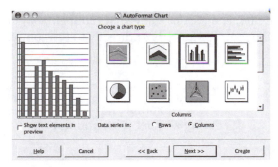

Select the labels:

(Continued)

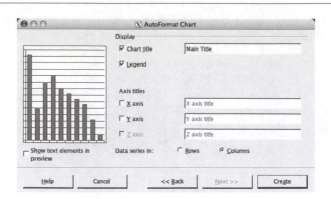

And save the chart. By default it will go into the current worksheet. The chart can be selected again later, and moved or modified. These charts can later be imported by other applications.

Spreadsheet software was covered first because, in some form, it is commonly available on desktop computers. In addition, spreadsheets are mostly quite easy to use. However, the appearance of charts is not under the control of the user to any great extent. Sometimes it is worthwhile to use other, more complicated, software packages such as **Matlab** (Mathworks), **IDL** (RSI), **Maple** (MapleSoft), **Canvas** (Deneba) or **Origin** (OriginLabs). These each include a command language that allows flexible control of the exact appearance of plots. With some effort, it is possible to create visually beautiful charts of data. Additionally, they also have sophisticated analysis tools built in. These applications are probably too expensive for home users, but one or more of them is frequently available at institutions. They are overkill for many data analysis projects, but for the remainder they are completely necessary.

One more example of a simple charting program is **gnuplot**, available free for Unix/Linux, Mac OS X, and Windows with Cygwin. It can be run interactively or from command files, and creates somewhat rudimentary plots, but is able to output in several different file formats or directly to the computer display.

Example
Creating a chart with gnuplot

Data file (indata):

10.0 3.0
11.0 4.0

```
15.0 4.2
16.0 4.9
17.0 6.3
18.0 8.1
```

Command file:

```
set term pbm small
set output 'plot.pbm'
set xlabel 'Distance'
set ylabel 'Size'
plot 'indata'
```

The resulting plot gets saved to (in this case) a PBM graphics format file called plot.pbm, which can be viewed with the **ImageMagick display** application in Linux, or the **Preview** application on Mac OS X, among others.

Resulting graph:

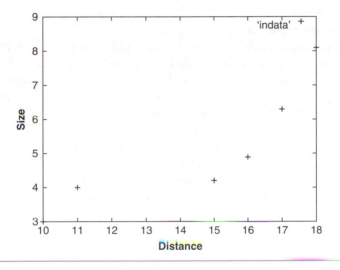

This is the simplest possible example of an x–y chart in **gnuplot**. More complicated charts, such as histograms or surface displays, are also possible with additional commands; and the size, font and locations of the labels can be controlled.

We started with data in tables of numbers, which can be plotted as x–y plots, histograms and scatter plots, but not all data come in this form. Other types of data are maps and graphs of relationships and connections.

Maps

Many types of data have a geographical component and are usefully displayed as maps. A few examples are: the incidence of cancers by region and their possible relation to environmental factors in the vicinity; the migration of ancient or modern populations across a region; voter preferences by county; and ethnic population distributions. Some studies involving mapping can be found in Lai and Mak (2007), Sinton and Lund (2007) and Knowles (2008).

The tools for displaying maps and associated data range from the very complete Geographic Information System (GIS) applications like **ArcGIS** from ESRI (http://esri.com/products.html), to open-source GIS applications like **GRASS** (http://grass.itc.it) and **OpenMap** (http://openmap.bbn.com), to other more general purpose applications that also draw maps such as **Canvas**, **Matlab** or **IDL**, and finally to web-based applications like **Google Maps**.

The term Geographic Information System arises because these applications allow the investigator to associate points on a map with other data. The professional packages like ArcGIS and the GIS component of **SAS** include a large collection of maps and locations, database management tools, and methods to analyze and display the information. Outside of these tools, there is a huge variety of map data available on the web. The book *Mapping Hacks* (Schuyler et al., 2005) is a useful starting point for the discovery of such data, and also of many interesting things that can be accomplished with geographic data. Their focus is mostly on open source software tools.

GIS programs like ArcGIS and others distinguish between three types of data: raster, vector and attribute. Raster data are a grid of values, for instance surface elevation or a scanned photograph, and are usually used as a background for the map. Vector data are also called shape data (particularly in ArcGIS), and includes points, lines and polygons. These are usually used to represent, for example, national boundaries, rivers, streets, buildings and city locations. Attributes are text and numbers that can be associated with a shape or vector item. Attributes are stored in a database format, and can be manipulated with database commands. A powerful feature of GIS systems is that as vector elements are combined or divided, the associated attributes are aggregated along with the vector elements, allowing for very sophisticated analysis of spatially organized data.

Another paradigm in many GIS programs is the use of layers, as similarly used in graphics tools like **Adobe Photoshop** and **GIMP**. All raster elements and vector elements are associated with a layer. The user can at any time select which layers to include in the analysis or display of the map. This way several different appearances can be generated from the same data.

ArcGIS

The ArcGIS tool comprises four products: **ArcReader**, **ArcView**, **ArcEditor** and **ArcInfo**. ArcReader is available as a free download from the ESRI web site and enables the viewing and printing of existing maps created with the more advanced tools. ArcView can be used to prepare maps and make queries about attribute data. ArcEditor includes additional data creation and editing tools, and ArcInfo includes others advanced spatial analysis tools. Each of the three advanced products actually consists of two applications on the computer: **ArcMap** and **ArcCatalog**, which handle specific tasks. The user interface is the same across all the products, so it is easy to move from one to the other.

Entire books have been written on GIS and tools like ArcGIS, so we can't begin to cover the topic, but we will examine a simple case of displaying a map with some user-provided data points, and suggest books such as *Getting to Know ArcGIS* (Ormsby, 2001) for a more in-depth description.

Example
Creating a Map Project in ArcGIS

Start the **ArcMap** application from **Start->All Programs->ArgGIS->ArcMap**. From the **ArcMap** dialog choose the **A new empty map** radio button.

Select the **Add Data** button
A file dialog will open, navigate to the ESRI->ESRIDATA->USA folder. Using Ctrl-Click to select multiple items, select COUNTIES.shp, LAKES.shp, Rivers.shp

and STATES.shp, and then click **Add**. A map of the whole United States will open and we'll need to zoom in on New England. In the tool palette select the **Zoom In** tool ⊕, and then click-drag the mouse to select the region you are interested in. You can do this multiple times until the correct

(Continued)

region is chosen. When finished selecting a region, choose the **Pointer** tool from the Tool palette ⬉. For safety, it is always a good idea to go back to the **Pointer** tool after finishing any operation because the **Pointer** does not cause any changes. Let us save this particular view, with **File->Save** from the main menu. The project will be saved with the name you select and a ".mxd" extension.

As you move the pointer around on the map, the latitude and longtitude of the pointer on the map are displayed on the lower bar of **ArcMap.**

Other charts

Some types of data are not amenable to usual chart styles; this is often especially true for qualitative data. Nevertheless it may still be useful to display the data with hierarchical tree displays, directed graphs or clustering.

Graphs of this type can be created manually in many applications like **Illustrator** (Adobe), **OmniGraffle** (Omni), and even in more general purpose programs such as presentation or word processing software. It is fairly straightforward; generally the process consists of choosing shape elements from a palette, manually positioning them on the page, and then selecting arrows from the pallet, and connecting the shapes. The process is, however, time-consuming, and can be annoyingly repetitive.

There is a freeware tool called **GraphViz** available for Windows, Mac OS X and Unix/Linux. GraphViz was developed by AT&T and is now available for download from http://graphviz.org. GraphViz uses a specialized text input language, which is interpreted to generate some fairly sophisticated graphs.

Example
Creating a directed graph with GraphViz

Input file:
```
digraph G {
 a -> b;
 a -> c;
 b -> c [ constraint=false ];
 b -> d;
 d -> b;
 c -> d;
```

}Resulting graph:

The GraphViz website has many examples of different types of graphs along with their input files. An input language like that of GraphViz can take some time to learn, but will eventually be much more convenient if used often.

Screen shots

Sometimes it is useful to get a graphic from the computer display into a document, when the graphic element is not from a file, or when the graphic element cannot be selected directly in the running application. For this eventuality, Windows, Mac OS X and the Linux each provide a screen shot facility.

In Windows, hitting the **Print Screen** key will save the contents of the display to the clipboard. Hitting **Alt+Print Screen** will save the contents of the front window to the clipboard, which is probably the more useful of the two. To refine the image further, it is necessary to paste the contents of the clipboard into a graphics application window. **Paint** is available in the **Programs->Accessories** menu, and is a minimal but adequate tool for this. **Paint** has a "crop" tool to select a rectangle within an image.

The Mac has more key combinations to select different parts of the display screen. There is a choice between saving screen shots to a file (called **Picture 1.png**, **Picture 2.png**, etc., in the user's Desktop), or to the clipboard for pasting into another application window. First, we list the save to a file commands. To save the whole screen to a file, hit **Apple+Shift+3** simultaneously. To save a chosen part of the screen to a file, hit **Apple+Shift+4**. A cross-hair symbol will appear at the cursor; use your mouse to drag the cursor across the rectangular area you want to save, and when you release the mouse button the area will be saved. To save a menu, dialog or window to a file, hit **Apple+Shift+4+Spacebar** (note the **4** and the

Spacebar are hit one after the other). A camera icon will appear at the cursor, move the cursor to the window you want to save, and click to save it. To modify each of these commands to save to the clipboard instead of to a file, add an additional **Ctrl** key to each of the above key sequences. To save the whole screen to the clipboard hit **Apple+Ctrl+Shift+3**. To save a screen area to the clipboard, hit **Apple+Ctrl+Shift+4**, then drag the cross-hair across the area to save. To save a menu, dialog or window to the clipboard, hit **Apple+Ctrl+Shift+4+Spacebar**, and click on the window to save.

In Linux it varies by the desktop choice, but there is usually an application available in the menu to save a screen shot to a file.

Including graphics in documents

Now that the graphics have been generated, we'll review how to insert them into document and presentation applications.

Presentations

Presentations to an audience, either live or online, often take the form of a slide show. The most commonly used software for this is **Microsoft Powerpoint**; some others are **OpenOffice Impress**, and **Apple Keynote**. They all make it very easy to create a computer-based slide show. Once in the application, the user creates one or more slides, and selects the appearance from a template of common types. Powerpoint offers the following choices.

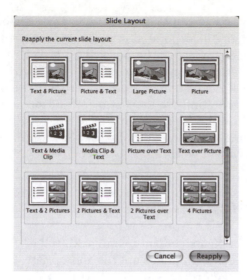

If chart or graphics are chosen, then the user can import either from an external source, whether that is a file or the system clipboard. These applications also include a table editor and graphing tool, so it is not really necessary to use a spreadsheet program at all. Generally, however, it is better to maintain data in a spreadsheet or other file format, rather than in the presentation itself.

When saving the presentation, one has the choice of saving it in native application format, or as a web document (HTML), or perhaps as a graphics file. If the presentation will be further manipulated, then save it in its native format. But if it will be distributed on the web, it is usually better to save it in a more readable format, either HTML or PDF. It is annoying for a potential viewer of the file to have access to the presentation document, but possibly not have the software to view it. Creating a PDF will take some additional steps from PowerPoint on Windows, but not on the Mac OS X version, nor on the Linux equivalents.

All the above presentation tools are impressive software packages, but all have two significant drawbacks. The presentations can only be viewed with the software package, which in some cases may not be available at the time or location of the presentation. Secondly, the saved files of the presentation are very large; which makes storage and transfer of the files inconvenient in some cases. There is an alternative, and that is to create the presentation directly in HTML mark-up language and view the presentation on any web browser. Web browsers are available on almost any computer these days. There is an open-source tool from the World Wide Web Consortium (W3C), called **Slidy** (http://www.w3.org/Talks/Tools/Slidy), which makes it a bit easier to create slide show type presentations directly into HTML. Slidy at present consists of a set of CSS (Cascading Style Sheets) and javascript instructions, which are incorporated into a web document with a URL link. Each slide of the document will be marked by a pair of matching HTML <div> and </div> tags. The presentation can be opened in a web browser either from the local file system or from a web site. The usual features of a computer slide presentation are then available: advancing with a space bar or page down button; backing up with page up; toggling full screen, etc. There is for the time being, no graphical application to create Slidy documents, so a standard text editor must be used.

Text documents

The majority of documents contain mainly text, rather than slides, tables or graphics. Text processing programs are the appropriate application for these, and can be **Microsoft Word**, **OpenOffice Writer**, **Apple Pages**, **Google Docs** and a range of others. Most journals in all fields of inquiry at present accept documents in Microsoft Word format, but in the physical sciences and mathematical sciences the preferred document format is based on the TeX typesetting language. This is because of the requirement for complicated formulas and plots that need to be very precise, both of which are fairly difficult to achieve in the standard word processing applications. However we will focus on the more usual applications.

Incorporating non-textual elements into a document can add to the effectiveness of the communication, and is fairly straightforward in all of the current word processing applications. Most will allow the importation of data from another program (tables or charts from a spreadsheet, for instance, or a graphics format file); and some incorporate their own methods for generating tables and various types of graphics. We'll cover a few cases in Microsoft Word.

As mentioned once before, in most cases it is advisable to keep data in a data document, and import the data into your presentation, rather than creating the data within your presentation. So the original data might be in a spreadsheet. To insert a table from an existing spreadsheet, select from the menu **Insert->Object** and then select the **From a File** tab (in Windows) or button (on Mac OS X). A file browser will allow you to then select the file. When you click **OK** the table will appear at the current cursor location of the document, looking something like the following.

1	21
2	24
3	33
4	34
5	28

6	25
7	21
8	17
9	12
10	7

If you want to create a one-off table right in place, without importing from another source, you can again make use of the **Insert** function. Chose from the menu **Table->Insert->Table**. In the **Insert table** dialog, choose the number of rows and columns, and optionally some fancy formatting, then click **OK**. This will create the grid (5 columns by 2 rows in the example). You can enter text into the table cells, as in the following example.

Africa	America	Asia	Australia	Europe
Big	Medium	Big	Small	Small

To insert a diagram, select from the menu **Insert->Diagram**. This will start up the **Microsoft Graph** application, and provide you with a list of chart types. Here we will choose an Organizational Chart, which we'll use to create a family tree. By default it creates one parent and three children. The appearance will be a bit different between the Windows and the Mac OS X versions. Click on each box to enter desired text. To add another element, click on one of the elements, and then, in the floating dialog, choose **Select->Branch**. Then click on **Insert Element** and a new shape will appear below the one selected (C1 below B1)

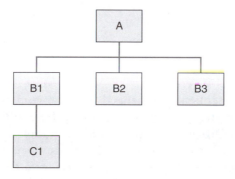

To insert a tabular chart, select from the menu **Insert->Picture->Chart**. A chart editor will pop up, and you can modify the contents or arrangements of the cells. After all the modifications are made and you hit **OK**, the chart will appear at the current cursor location.

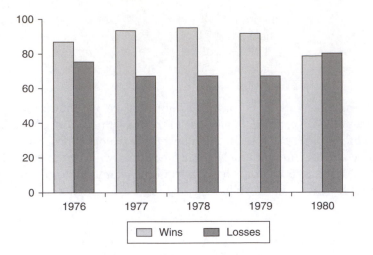

To modify the chart after the initial creation, right-click anywhere on the chart; then in the pop-up menu select **Chart Object->Open**. This will open up **Microsoft Graph**, and show the contents of the cells and the chart. Enter text into the datasheet to change the values, or right-click on the chart and select **Chart Options** to change labels and other appearance variables. Select **File-> Update** in the Graph window and then close it.

Very fine online tutorials are available at http://inpics.net for the **Microsoft Office 2003** and **Office 2007** applications and the **OpenOffice 2** applications; and, additionally, **Adobe Dreamweaver** and **Adobe Photoshop** and some web technologies. These are step-by-step guides that lead the user through various aspects of each program. More tutorials on current applications are in the works.

File formats

All document or graphics creation applications save their files in a particular format. When documents are exchanged between computers, the choice of format sometimes creates difficulties when compatible software is not present. Since the **Microsoft Office** applications are so common in the desktop world, there is a tendency for some people to distribute documents in the **Office** native application formats. But this has an expectation that the recipient will have the appropriate application to read the file, and this may not be the case.

The document format is often known by letters of the filename extension used on Windows. For example, MS Word saves files with a ".doc" extension to the file name, so the MS Word default document format is knows as "DOC" format. Similarly, the default MS Excel format is "XLS" and the default MS Powerpoint format is called "PPT". Note that these file name extensions may or may not be visible in the Windows File Explorer window, depending on whether the user has checked "Hide extension for known file types" in the Explorer folder options. The Windows operating system relies on these extensions to associate the document with the application used to create it or view it. However, **MS Word 95** and **MS Word 2003** both use the ".doc" extension even though the file types are not compatible; **Word 95** cannot read a file saved by **Word 2003** in the default format.

The file name extension is also used by email applications, on Windows as well as on Mac OS X and Linux, to properly encode the document for inclusion in an email message. Difficulties in exchanging documents by sending the document as an email attachment between computers running Windows and computers running other systems are sometimes caused by failing to use the appropriate name extension on the document file.

As mentioned previously, when a document file is transferred to another computer, the other computer needs to have appropriate software to read the document. Hopefully it has the very same application as used to create it, but it is often not the case. **Microsoft Office** is a fairly expensive application suite and may be beyond the recipient's budget. **OpenOffice** is able to read Microsoft Office documents for the most part, so that might be one option for the recipient. Both Office and OpenOffice are very large applications that take a lot of disk space and memory. With modern computers this is not often a problem, but older computers may not even be able to handle either of these document types.

If the document is intended to be read and not modified, a better choice would be to save it in Adobe's portable document format (PDF) and transmit that. Of course PDF files need an appropriate application to read it as well, but **Adobe Reader** is available for download for free from the Adobe web site, and is available for Windows, Mac OS X and Unix/Linux. Mac OS X has a built-in program called **Preview** that displays PDF files, so Adobe Reader is not even necessary, though it does have some features beyond those that Preview has. Users of Unix and Linux can usually install **xpdf**, or **gv,** or some other option to view PDF files. The Microsoft Office applications do not by themselves have an option to save as PDF, but if the full version of **Adobe Acrobat** is installed, then it adds buttons to the Office applications to save in PDF format. An open-source application called **PDFCreator** (http://sourceforge.net/projects/pdfcreator/) can also add this capability. On Mac OS X, PDF is considered a native file format, so all applications on Mac OS X can save to PDF – it is part of the Print menu. **OpenOffice** and **Google Docs** also have the option of saving to PDF. However, there are few applications outside of Adobe Acrobat that can modify a PDF file, so that should be considered if the file needs to be further edited. Starting with the Vista operating system, Microsoft is promoting a portable document format it calls XPS. It has many of the same advantages as Adobe's PDF format in terms of preserving the appearance of documents, but at this point it is only available on the Microsoft platform, so it is not as generally useful.

Many of Microsoft's competitors like OpenOffice.org, Corel and IBM/Lotus have standardized on a document format called the **Open Document Format (ODF)**. There is a movement in governments to support ODF, because of some issues they face in being able to read documents over a long period of time, past the time when applications become outdated and obsolete. Microsoft naturally opposes standardization on a file format not used by its applications, and has proposed its own file formats as a different standard it calls **OOXML (Office Open XML** – not to be confused with OpenOffice). This is the default format for **MS Office 2007**, and the file name extensions are "docx", "xlsx" and "pptx". This format has partial, but not complete approval at this point in time by the international standards bodies. The conflict between ODF and OOXML is currently a political battle. Eventually there will be some plug-ins so that applications supporting the Open Document Format can read the Office Open XML formats.

A well-done presentation is very satisfying; regrettably not everyone puts much effort into the visual appearance of presentations. Charts and graphs can be excellent aids, but should be simple and concise. Different graphics applications have different strengths, and the researcher should consider a variety of graphics tools. Once created in any application, it is a simple matter to copy a graphic to the presentation, whether it is a text document, auditorium slide show, or web document.

12 SOME ADDITIONAL CHALLENGES FOR ONLINE RESEARCHERS

Chapter summary

- To lurk or not to lurk?
- The meaning of privacy in the online environment
- Private or public?
- The meaning of ownership online
- What does it mean to be a virtual persona?
- Conducting research with minors

Throughout this book we've tried to offer practical tips and illustrations to assist you in your online research endeavors. We feel that we've gathered a great deal of information in this one location, but also know that in some respects we have barely scratched the surface. There are too many applications, too many techniques, and too many individualized nuances in online research for us to cover comprehensively every last detail. It is our intention that this book will become a point of reference for you in your research, and serve as a beginner's guide as you venture into the world of online research.

In the same way that there are many software applications and research techniques, there are also many subtleties in the online environment. While we've covered many aspects in the sections on designing your research, particularly in the section addressing ethical issues, there are, of course, many other things we could say about conducting research online. Before concluding this book, though, we would like to offer a few more considerations unique to the online environment. It is our thought that these topics do not lend themselves to a particular method, but rather speak more broadly about research in the virtual world. In any event, we want to share them with you, our reader, before bringing this project to a close.

Lurking/deception

An issue that often gets discussed in the context of online research is that of "lurking." As noted in Wikipedia (http://en.wikipedia.org/wiki/Lurker, accessed on 11 April 2007):

> The term dates back to the mid-1980s, when most people did not have access to the internet, but used BBS chat rooms and message boards instead.
>
> Because BBSs were often accessed by a single phone line (frequently in someone's home), there was an expectation that all who used a bulletin board would contribute to its content by uploading files and posting comments. Lurkers were viewed negatively, and might be barred from access by the sysop, if they did not contribute anything but kept the phone line tied up for extended periods.
>
> Many internet communities advise newbies to lurk for some time to get a feel for the specific culture and etiquette of the community, lest they make an inappropriate or redundant comment, ask a frequently asked question, or incite a flame war.

This statement from a Wikipedia entry highlights the broadness of this issue. Many lurker types are noted, and yet none of them applies directly to a researcher. In the case of a researcher, the major issues are related to being "present" but silent, and gathering information for the purposes of research and analysis without the knowledge and consent of the participants. Lurking, in this sense, is a type of participant observation. As such, discipline-specific research guidelines should be a source of advice and recommendations relative to study design.

When thinking about the issue of lurking, it's useful to keep in mind that there are certain assumptions being made by those in an online environment. People often assume a kind of trust relative to their involvement in an online community. Part of that trust is that they are all participating for the same reason, be it self-help, to play together, or to discuss a particular topic. Since the online environment makes it possible to enter a space anonymously, to be present and use the interaction and words for purposes other than what is stated as normative for the community is a violation of group trust.

As Barbara Sharf (1999: 246) notes, "an email communiqué from one person to another is analogous to a letter or phone call, ostensibly private, but capable of interception." To illustrate, although it is possible to take the mail out of your box and read it, I don't. Most of us believe that our mail is private, whether or not it is against the law to take it. Given this is the standard perception, what leads us to believe that it is okay to read and use someone's online mail without their permission? The question is one of social expectation. Isn't it fair to assume the same level of social expectation for online communication?

One of the potential problems researchers face in using data they accessed without permission is the accusation of exploitation (Sharf, 1999: 248). Some people who may be in particularly vulnerable personal places, such as those exploring their sexuality or participating in self-help groups, might feel violated and quite angry that they are being taken advantage of while in a state of distress when/if it becomes known that their interactions are being studied without their knowledge or permission (ibid.: 250).

One way that a researcher might address concerns regarding lurking, or, as stated previously, exploitation, would be to seek permission after the fact. While this enables you to analyze, write, publish and present with a relatively clean conscience, it's entirely possible that participants will be less than excited with your request for approval. It's likely that some will be hostile, and may refuse their permission. This situation could leave you in a bind as you try to meet deadlines, complete your study and submit it for publication.

There is an added dilemma to the concern about reading someone's online exchanges without their permission that compounds the ethical challenge. The environment lends itself to a higher level of self-disclosure due to the sense of anonymity online (Sharf, 1999: 246). Arguably, lurking with this knowledge could be construed as taking advantage of individuals who are vulnerable.

To be clear, the point here is not to suggest that it is never acceptable to lurk, but rather for you, the researcher, to be intentional and thoughtful about when, where and how you choose to do so. There are times when it might be appropriate to lurk before interacting with participants. As Lori Kendall (1999) indicates, if you disclose too soon that you are lurking you may bias responses or constrain group interaction. However, as stated previously, the intent in lurking should not be to deceive or violate trust, but rather to use it strategically to gather data that you can then use appropriately to communicate with participants as to your intentions and interests. For example, by being a lurker you might learn something interesting about how people cluster and form in groups to play an online game. When you ask for consent, you could share with the participants what you've learned, indicating why it was valuable for you to lurk, and why you are hoping they will give their consent so that you can share what you learned with others.

Privacy

The distinction between 'privacy' and 'lurking' is a bit arbitrary. In many ways they are relative issues. The privacy debate is related to individuals wanting the right to "surf" the internet without someone tracking the details of where they go, what they do, who they associate with, and so forth. In recent public debates, governments have claimed the right to review search engine records for purposes of public safety. While it is difficult to argue the right of a terrorist to use the internet to learn how to build a bomb, or the right of a sexual predator to search for and exchange child pornography, it is equally difficult to consider that political activity or an adult's consensual engagement in what some might consider sexually deviant behavior could also be monitored. It is possible that the line in this debate will continue to shift for years to come.

What is important in the privacy debate is that researchers consider their actions when working online in light of current social norms. It's useful to ask yourself some questions such as "Is it okay to have any kind of identifier in your findings?" or "When using data from a databank is a researcher responsible for ensuring that any identifiable information is stripped from the data before these are used?" We believe it is safe to assume that the responses to these questions are not absolute and will continue to evolve in the public conscience. Political debate, economic behavior, military action, use of the internet, new technologies that transform our understanding of the internet are all among the social forces that will continue to impact our thinking and understanding of online privacy. There are many permutations to this debate too numerous to author here. We commend Buchanan (2004) and Mann and Stewart (2000) to you as good places to seek assistance when considering privacy issues.

Public and private spaces

One difficulty in online research is determining what is and what isn't a private or public space. Many people believe that there are no private spaces online. Others, however, feel that there is a line between public and private spaces, and that people should respect each other's space. Again, this is a debate with shifting boundaries, likely to continue for years to come.

As noted by some researchers (e.g. King, 1996), some participants have an expectation of privacy in online venues that should be honored. Other researchers (e.g. Herring, 1996), on the other hand, feel it is acceptable to consider all computer-mediated communication to be public. We tend to agree with the former perspective in honoring the expectation of privacy. We encourage you to exercise some element of care and consideration when selecting environments in which you choose to conduct your research and how you go about collecting data. Likewise, use the same care and thoughtfulness as you consider when and how to seek informed consent. Ultimately, we encourage all researchers to exercise judgment when entering new spaces and when deciding whether or not to consider an online space public.

Ownership

Related to public and private spaces is the issue of ownership. Who owns what in the online environment can be a complex issue for online researchers. While it may seem obvious to many readers, we can assure you it is not. To illustrate the point, consider the following research example. In a study conducted by one of us, a participant indicated that she, too, was a researcher and, as such, automatically was a co-researcher and co-author of anything produced from the study. She believed that since her participation was textual, she had ownership of her words as an author would own the copyright to a publication. This issue raises the question that if I participate in a study, typing my comments in an email or on your listserv, do I retain copyright to my words, or do I forfeit my copyright by agreeing to participate in your study? If I post my experience on a bulletin board or in a blog, do I retain copyright of something I "published" online, or does my posting online make my experience public information and therefore subject to fair use?

When attempting to determine ownership, it is unclear whether a posting is owned by the author, the community where it was posted or sent, or anyone who has access to it in some manner (Roberts, Smith & Pollock, 2004). If we look to legal experts regarding copyright, we are likely to hear about issues such as "Implied License", whereby it is assumed that whoever posted the message has granted an implied license to others to at least make copies of that information (Smedinghoff, 1996c). Implied license, however, does not clarify the question of ownership as much as it simply provides a structure for granting permission to use online information.

Implicit in the discussion of ownership is how we, as researchers, attribute information. If we state something like "according to Schreiner," we naturally provide data that attribute the comments to a particular author. If we include a reference from Wikipedia, we have a standard by which we give a web address and date of access, attributing the information to the web-based encyclopedia. So it stands to reason that if we read a personal blog we might consider providing the same authorship. As with other issues, the question is where to draw the line. Is there a difference in attributing authorship between a lengthy email and a blog? Is this an issue that we can simply address in informed consent or in the opening pages of research findings, making clear when we are and aren't going to identify authorship?

Ownership questions continue to evolve as our use and understanding of online environments continue to develop. As online interaction becomes more mainstream, it is safe to assume that legal scholars will play a greater role in determining how we should handle many of these types of issues. In the meantime, researchers are encouraged to exercise judgment and to be clear with research participants about their working definition of what constitutes ownership.

Use of a virtual persona (Second Life, chat environments, deception, etc.)

Virtual personae represent a new and unique challenge in the online environment. As we write this book, researchers are beginning to venture into Second Life, where individuals can create an alter ego, a virtual persona that represents them in whatever way they would like to be represented. In this environment, does "virtual Tom" directly represent "real-life Tom?" Does it matter? Do we, as researchers, attribute contributions to "virtual Tom" or "real-life Tom?"

As in other discussions, the distinction between "virtual Tom" and "real-life Tom" may seem obvious to some, yet it can be more complicated than it initially appears. To take a simple example, let's say a researcher is studying family dynamics and chooses to do so through the use of focus groups or interviews. Looking for a collection of diverse participants, she goes into Second Life and sets up shop. She, herself, is now represented by a "virtual researcher" persona. This persona recruits and asks questions of "virtual Tom." She asks basic questions related to roles and responsibilities in the household. She finishes, and "virtual Tom" is then met by "virtual Jane," his Second Life wife. In this moment, the researcher realizes that it is entirely possible that his responses were about his virtual wife and not his real-life wife. It's possible that she was interested in virtual life relationships. It's possible that she might be able to research both. It's possible that she might want to design a study to compare and contrast relationships in the virtual world with terrestrial relationships by recruiting participants that inhabit both worlds. The point is that it isn't clear what and who "virtual Tom" represents. Therefore, researchers will need to continue to explore the challenges posed by virtual personae as they expand their research endeavors into the virtual spaces inhabited by virtual beings.

Electronic research and minors

The online environment has become a hang-out, of sorts, for youth. Students go online to do research, teenagers blog about teen issues, and many young people go online to meet new people, explore their budding sense of self, and engage in interactive games. The point is that when researching online, a researcher is just as likely to encounter a teenager as an adult. When teens are study participants, there are additional research concerns to consider. As Susannah Stern (2004) notes, the primary issues involve not only getting parental consent, and but also the responsibility of a researcher who encounters a distressing disclosure by a young person.

In some instances parental consent may be considered necessary, and would be in an offline research experience. However, the online environment and the teens themselves may constrain access to parents. The way a researcher might decide whether or not parental consent is warranted could depend on whether or not the space used by a particular young person is considered private or public. As Stern notes, however, young people often have a different perspective on what is and isn't private, making this distinction difficult. A teen, for example, might assume that anything not meant for anyone other than friends is private, even though it is posted on the internet in a public manner (Stern, 2004). Thus, the understanding of whether or not a space is considered "private" could impact a researcher's decision of whether or not to pursue parental consent.

Mann and Stewart (2000: 53) note that the challenges and ethical difficulty of researching children "whose maturity, personality, and possible vulnerabilities may be unknown," pretty much necessitates recruiting and securing consent through adult guardians. They further suggest that to ensure that you are communicating with the correct person, it is a good idea to consider obtaining consent in paper format (ibid.). This limits the pool of participants, but may be the most appropriate solution for including minors in online research.

Whether or not parental consent is warranted, there is another constraint: access. While a researcher may feel an obligation to seek parental consent, access to parents must come through the young people themselves. Since the online environment enables youthful independence, it is unlikely that many people will want to seek parental consent for their engagement online. Stern (2004) notes that this has been the case in her own work and that of others. Ultimately, she suggests that if parental consent is desired for a study, the optimal way to recruit and get consent is offline. This, however, changes the nature of an online study by providing a real world link between participant and researcher, constraining recruitment.

Concluding comments

Reflecting on the issues outlined in the preceding pages, along with other research design comments in earlier chapters, we hope that we have given you sufficient information to begin to navigate the ever-changing waters of online research. At the very least, we assume we have provided you with the sense that there are no hard and fast rules. The environment continues to change, presenting us with new opportunities for research. We also suggest that as the environment continues to change, we, too, are being changed along with it. As we change, and virtual environments continue to transform, the challenges for conducting research in these new spaces will persist. Our approach has been to provide you with some practical skills and tips to help you tame what some might feel is a technological beast.

To some, the online environment as a shifting research environment may feel daunting. We believe, though, that it offers an exciting shift in the possibilities for research and provides a wealth of opportunity. For example, when we think of research we typically think of researcher and participant. The internet, however, appears to be transforming the role of researcher and those being researched. While shifting roles may become increasingly challenging, some of the challenges noted in the preceding pages, such as the line between public and private, ownership, authorship, and so forth, may decrease in importance with each passing day.

As we continue to struggle with these issues and mature in our online research techniques, all of our definitions and understandings of the environment and its inhabitants will continue to evolve. Given that we believe this is the future, it is our hope that this book will help many readers to embrace the change in preparation for the research activities of tomorrow.

APPENDIX 1 – ACRONYMS AND JARGON TERMS

Apache – A commonly used open source web server application. (See also Server, Open Source.)

ASCII – American Standard Code for Information Interchange. A coding method used to store letters, numbers, and certain punctuation marks in computer memory. ASCII consists of 128 symbols, and includes the US English character set and the most used punctuation marks, basically the characters available on a US keyboard. Accented characters, other alphabets and various symbols such as non-US currency symbols are not part of the ASCII code set.

Blog – Short for Weblog, a web site where one, or a small number of contributors publish journal entries. Articles are usually displayed in reverse chronological order. Many blog sites allow readers to comment on the articles.

CGI – Common Gateway Interface. A standard for sending information from a web browser back to programs on a web server, by way of such items in web page forms as checkboxes, menu list choices, text entry boxes, and others.

Client – A computer or a computer application that is used to send or receive information, by communicating with a server. (See also, Server.)

CMS – Content Management System. A set of applications on a server that helps organize a content site, which is most often a blog, wiki or other type of web site.

CSS – Cascading Style Sheet. A syntax for controlling the positioning and appearance of elements on a web page. The functionality overlaps with HTML, but typically HTML is used to specify the text and image content, and CSS is used to specify the position and attributes such as color, font, and size of the content.

CSV – Comma-separated Variable List. A text file where data or variable fields on each line are separated from each other by a comma character. CSV is a lowest common denominator file format and it is often used to move data between incompatible applications.

Digest – An aggregation of messages. Many mail list servers may be set to send only a once-a-day digest of messages instead of sending each message separately. The digest option can usually be requested individually by a user.

DNS – Domain Name System. A protocol and set of servers that translates human-oriented server names such as mail.google.com into their numerical addresses, which are used by the network routing systems.

Ethnography – The observation, study and description of organizations and small societies.

Feed – A supply of data to a system, but most often used as a data format for providing users with frequently updated content. Users may subscribe to a feed to receive its content. (See also, RSS.)

Flaming – Deliberately hostile communication in a forum, chat list or mailing list. It is often a response to new users not conforming to the conventions of the forum, but may simply be hostile disagreement to someone's statement.

FTP – File Transfer Protocol. A protocol for the uploading and downloading of files from a remote computer system. Transmission is usually unencrypted or "in the clear", so it is potentially possible for snoopers to gather passwords if they are sent. Many data provider sites offer anonymous FTP for download whereby clients may connect without using any log in (See also, SCP.)

GIS – Geographic Information System. An application or set of applications that handles map data, including feature outlines and attribute information to geographic features.

HTML – HyperText Markup Language. The language standard that web browsers use to interpret and display web pages. (See also, CSS, CGI, HTTP.)

HTTP – HyperText Transfer Protocol. The protocol to control communication between web servers and web browsers. (See also, CGI, HTML.)

IM – Instant Messaging. A communication method, usually between computers, but also with advanced telephones, where messages appear directly on the receiving system if it is logged in.

IMAP – Internet Message Access Protocol. One of the mail client protocols used to retrieve users' mail from a mail server. Mail messages are usually left on the server. (See also, POP, SMTP.)

IRC – Internet Relay Chat. One of the methods used to provide multi-user instant messaging or chat.

ISP – Internet Service Provider. A company or organization that provides access to users to the internet.

Log Files – Files created by applications that list actions taken by the application. For instance, web servers maintain logs of all page requests, and instant messaging clients optionally maintain logs of conversations. Log files are often text and easily analyzed with appropriate tools, but sometime logs need to explicitly exported to text files before they can be analyzed.

Lurking – Being a member of a forum or mailing list to observe but without contributing to the discussion. Lurkers may often just do so until they become comfortable with contributing and then become active participants.

Mailman – A commonly used open source mailing list server application. (See also, Open Source.)

MAPI – Messing Application Programming Interface. A messaging architecture which is used by some Microsoft applications to communicate with the Microsoft Exchange server.

MIME – Multipurpose Internet Mail Extensions. A standard way to encode non-text files such as images, audio files and executable files before transmission over protocols that only allow transmission of text data. It is used by mail servers and web servers.

MMORPG – Massive Multi-player Online Role-Playing Game. An on-line role-playing game environment with a large number of participants. These environments are usually hosted at a commercial site and require client software to connect and participate. (See also, RPG. Client.)

MOO – MUD Object Oriented. An enhancement of the MUD comcept that allows users to program their environment, possibly changing the behavior of the environment. (See also, MUD.)

MUD – Multi-user Dungeon (or Domain). A multi-player on-line role-playing game with the features of a chat room. Players interact with each other using text commands. (See also, MOO, RPG.)

ODF – Open Document Format. A file format used by OpenOffice, IBM and others to store data from office productivity applications. (See also, OOXML, PDF.)

OOXML – Office Open XML. A file format used by Microsoft to store the data from Office applications like Word, Excel and Powerpoint, starting with the 2007 version. (See also, ODF, PDF.)

Open Source – a programming philosophy and also a licensing mode that requires distributed software to be made available in its source form so that users may examine the code, and under some restrictions, also modify it. Most, but not all, of the GNU/Linux operating system is open source.

PDF – Portable Document Format. A file format used originally by Adobe to create visually accurate document files. PDF files are usually the best way to distribute files where the appearance needs to be closely controlled. There are many applications that can display PDF files, but few applications that can modify PDF files once created, so they are usually considered read-only documents.

Perl – A scripting language with powerful features for text handling, often used in association with web server CGI programs. Perl is a very terse language and somewhat difficult to learn, but very powerful. (See also, CGI, PHP, Python, Ruby.)

PHP – A web page programming language. PHP programs can be embedded in web pages to provide dynamic behavior. PHP is distinguished from the Perl and Python languages in that the web server usually interprets the PHP code to generate the resulting output instead of calling a separated program to execute the script. PHP is quite easy to learn. (See also, HTML, CGI, Perl, Python, Ruby.)

POP – Post-Office Protocol, One of the mail client protocols used to retrieve users' mail from a mail server. Mail messages are typically downloaded to the client and deleted from the server. (See also, IMAP, SMTP.)

Python – A scripting language with powerful features for text handling, often used in association with web server CGI programs. Python is fairly easy to learn and has features to help ensure correctness, yet is very powerful. (See also, CGI, Perl, PHP, Ruby.)

RDB – Relational Database. A file or set of files that organizes data in rows and columns and also provides a way to set up links or relations to other files. Relational databases can usually be accessed and modified at much higher rates than text files, so are useful as storage systems for other applications.

RDBMS – Relational Database Management System. An application or set of applications that provides access to a relational database.

RPG – Role-Playing Game. A game in which players assume fantasy roles. Many of these games are played over a communication network, where they may be conducted with simple text commands an responses or with sophisticated graphics. (See also, MUD, MMORPG.)

RSS – Really Simple Syndication (and other expansions). A family of formats used to publish frequently updated content or data, such as news headlines and blog site entries. The RSS formats are usually written in XML. (See also, Blog, Feed, XML.)

Ruby - A scripting language with powerful features for text handling, often used in association with web server CGI programs. (See also, CGI, Perl, PHP, Python.)

SCP – Secure Shell Copy. A component of SSH, but used for transferring files rather than interactive login sessions. Preferable to other file transfer methods such as FTP because the transmission of passwords is encrypted to discourage snooping. (See also, SSH, FTP.)

Server – A computer or a computer application that maintains data and communicates with a client which initiates transfers from, or to the server. (See also, Client.)

Shape File – A computer file containing a set coordinate points for a geographic information system, used to store map features. (See also, GIS.)

SLA – Service Level Agreement. An agreement between a provider of services and a client, which specifies thing such as availability, response time, customer support and even pricing for the services.

SMTP – Simple Mail Transfer Protocol. The protocol most widely used by mail servers to communicate with each other when transferring mail messages. (See also, IMAP, POP.)

SQL – Structured Query Language. A standardized computer language, used to access relational databases. It includes commands for inserting, selecting and updating data within the file. (See also RDB, RDBMS.)

SSH – Secure Shell. A method and an application for logging in to remote server systems. Transmission is encrypted so that snoopers and unintended listeners cannot intercept passwords. (See also, SCP.)

Threaded Discussion – A mail list server or forum discussion where the messages are grouped together by subject. Some mail clients have support to display related messages next to each other.

URL – Uniform Resource Locator. A standard text representation of a file location on a web server, typically used within HTML links. (See also, HTML.)

Usenet – A network of computer servers that maintains and provides access to news lists. The Usenet is one of the original on-line forums.

Wiki – A web site where a large or select number of users can generate content, but also edit previously entered content. Wikis are often used as knowledge repositories.

WYSIWYG – What You See Is What You Get. Many file content editors and word processing applications can show the appearance of the resulting page as it is being edited. Other (usually older) application show the literal contents of a document including the page markup, but require a separate application to show the actual appearance. There are advantages to both methods.

XML – Extensible Markup Language. A language consisting of tags, attributes and values, often used to store application data or to exchange data between applications. XML is called extensible because it allows for the definition of new tags to describe new properties. (See also, RSS.)

APPENDIX 2 – WEB LINKS

Chapter 1.
http://en.wikipedia.org/wiki/Email
http://www.martketingterms.com/dictionary/blog/
http://en.wikipedia.org/wiki/MUD
http://secondlife.com
http://www.cdc.gov/datastatistics/
http://www.imf.org/external/data.htm
http://www.worldbank.org
http://www.hhs.gov/ocr/hipaa/
http://memory.loc.gov/learn/start/cite/index.html
http://en.wikipedia.org/wiki/cyberspace

Chapter 2.
http://www.loc.gov/exhibits/treasures/trm145.html
http://www.nic.fi/~mauvinen/mircstats/mircstatsfaq.html#multifiles
http://www.surveymonkey.com
http://www.sla-zone.co.uk

Chapter 3.
http://www.mra-net.org/pdf/expanded_code.pdf
http://www.asanet.org/page.ww?section=Ethics&name=Code+of+Ethics+Standards#9
http://onlineethics.org/reseth/index.html
http://www.mra-net.org/pdf/expanded_code.pdf
http://www.asanet.org/cs/root/leftnav/ethics/code_of_ethics_table_of_contents/
http://www.apa.org/science/standards.html
http://www.srcd.org/ethicalstandards.html
http://www.ethicsweb.ca/resources/research/
http://TRFN.pgh.pa.us/guest/mrtext.html
http://www2000.ogsm.vanderbilt.edu/cyberporn.debate.cgi
http://www.bitlaw.com/copyright/fair_use.html
http://www.bitlaw.com/copyright/license.html
http://www2.asanet.org/members/ecostand2.html

Chapter 4.
http://en.wikipedia.org/wiki/Comparison_of_e-mail_clients
http://en.wikipedia.org/wiki/Comparison_of_webmail_providers
http://www.mozilla.org
http://www.gnu.org/software/mailman/

http://www.lsoft.com/products/listserv.asp
htto://www.greatcircle.com/majordomo/
http://www.xequte.com/maillistking/
http://groups.yahoo.com
http://groups.msn.com/home/
http://www.simplelists.com
http://www.webpronews.com/ebusiness/contentandcopywriting/wpn-6-20050727EmailInterviews.html

Chapter 5.
http://en.wikipedia.org/wiki/Comparison_of_instant_messaging_clients
http://www.mirc.com/
http://www.xchat.org/
http://www.pidgin.im/
http://www.adiumx.com
http://www.mozilla.org/projects/rt-messaging/chatzilla/
http://www.irchelp.org/irchelp/irctutorial.html
http://www.ircd-hybrid.org

Chapter 6.
http://sourceforge.net/phpesp
http://www.educara.com/educara.cgi/products
http://www.psychdata.net
http://www.surveypro.com
http://www.surveymonkey.com
http://www.surveysaid.com

Chapter 7.
http://en.wikipedia.org/wiki/Web_2.0
http://www.democratic-conversation.com/
http://dailykos.com
http://www.triplebranch.blogspot.com/
http://gizmodo.com
http://www.captainsquartersblog.com/mt/archives/009354.php
http://technorati.com
http://icerocket.com
http://blogarama.com
http://del.icio.us
http://wordpress.org/
http://www.typepad.com
http://www.moveabletype.org
http://www.blogger.com
http://www.blogsome.com
http://www.wikipedia.com
http://www.mediawiki.org/wiki/MediaWiki
http://moinmoin.wikiwikiweb.de
http://www.wikia.com/wiki/Wikia
http://www.wetpaint.com
http://www.bloglines.com

Chapter 8.
http://www.socio.com
http://www.phpmyadmin.net/home_page/index.php
http://awstats.sourceforge.net
http://www.mrunix.net/webalizer/
http://www.analog.cx/
http://www.llrx.com/columns/stats.htm
http://web.worldbank.org/WBSITE/EXTERNAL/DATASTATISTICS/0,,men
uPK:232599~pagePK:64133170~piPK:64133498~theSitePK:239419,00.html
http://www.imf.org/external/data.htm
http://support.microsoft.com/kb/307877

Chapter 9.
http://www.socresonline.org.uk/socresonline/3/3/4.html
http://www.researchware.com
http://www.qsrinternational.com/products_nvivo.aspx
http://www.atlasti.com
http://www.qualisresearch.com
http://www.maxqda.com
http://www.qsrinternational.com/support_tutorials.aspx
http://www.reasearchware.com/hr/downloads.html
http://caqdas.soc.surrey.ac.uk
http://www.quarc.de/body_overview.html
http://www.stattransfer.com

Chapter 10.
http://www.orgnet.com/sna.html
http://www.orgnet.com/inflow3.html
http://www.insna.org/INSNA/soft_inf.html
http://www.insna.org/indexConnect.html
http://www.mpogd.com
http://secondlife.com
http://pacec-sped.org/pf6007.htm
http://www.bc.edu/bc_org/avp/law/st_org/iptf/commentary/content/
1999060506.html

Chapter 11.
http://www.esri.com/products.html
http://grass.itc.it
http://openmap.bbn.com
http://graphviz.org
http://www.w3.org/Talks/Tools/Slidy
http://www.inpics.net
http://sourceforge.net/projects/pdfcreator

Chapter 12.
http://en.wikipedia.org/wiki/Lurker

BIBLIOGRAPHY

Adobe Systems, Inc. (2002) *Adobe Photoshop: Classroom in a Book*. www.adobe.com/adobepress.

Babbie, E. (2007) *The Practice of Social Research*. 11th ed. Belmont, CA: Thomas Wadsworth Publishing.

Bakardjieva, M. (2005) *Internet Society: The Internet in Everyday Life*. London: Sage Publications.

Barry, C.A. (1998) Choosing Qualitative Data Analysis Software: Atlas/ti and Nudist Compared. *Sociological Research Online*. vol. 3. no. 3. www.socresonline.org.uk/socresonline/3/3/4.html.

Bell, D. (2001) *An Introduction to Cybercultures*. New York, NY: Routledge.

Berk, K. and Carey, P. (2000) *Data Analysis with Microsoft Excel*. Pacific Grove, CA: Duxbury.

Best, S. and Krueger, R.S. (2004) *Internet Data Collection*. Thousand Oaks, CA: Sage Publications.

Bishop, E.L. (1993) *Tinker, Taylor, Soldier – Why?: Renegotiating the Employment Relation When Organizations Introduce Computer Networks*. Dissertation, University of California, Berkeley. UMI Publication Number AAT 9430395.

Blank, G., Fielding, N. and Lee, R. (2008) *Handbook of Online Research Methods*. London: Sage Publications.

Bowman, J., Emerson, S.L. and Darnovsky, M. (2001) *The Practical SQL Handbook: Using SQL Variants*. Reading, MA: Addison-Wesley.

Buchanan, E. (2004) *Readings in Virtual Research Ethics: Issues and Controversies*. Hershey, PA: Information Science Publishing.

Buchanan, R.A. (1992) *The Power of the Machine: The Impact of Technology From 1700 to the Present*. New York, NY: Penguin Books.

Burnett, B. and Roberts, A. (2005) in P. Comeaux (ed.) *Assessing Online Learning*. Bolton, MA: Anker.

Busiel, C. and Maeglin, T. (1998) *Researching Online*. New York, NY: Longman.

Castells, M. (2000) *The Rise of the Network Society*. vol.1. Malden, MA: Blackwell.

Charalabidis, A. (1999) *The Book of IRC: The Ultimate Guide to Internet Relay Chat*. San Francisco, CA: No Starch Press.

Cherny, L. (1999) *Conversations and Community: Chat in a Virtual World*. Stanford, CA: CSLI Publications.

Clodius, J. (1994) Ethnographic Fieldwork on the Internet. *Anthropology Newsletter*, 35 (December), 9.

Coiro, J., Knobel, M., Lankshear, C. and Leu, D.J. (eds.) (2008) *Handbook of Research on New Literacies*. New York, NY: Lawrence Erlbaum Associates.

Comeaux, P. (ed.) (2005) *Assessing Online Learning*. Bolton, MA: Anker Publishing Company.

Davis B. and Brewer J. (1997) *Electronic discourse: linguistic individuals in virtual space*. Albany, NY: State University of New York Press.

Diener, E. and Crandall, R. (1978) *Ethics in Social and Behavioral Research*. Chicago, IL: University of Chicago Press.

Dubrovsky, V., Kiesler, S. and Sethna. B. (1991) The Equalization Phenomenon: Status Effects in Computer-Mediated and Face-to-Face Decision Making Groups. *Human Computer Interaction*. 6. pp. 199–146.

Eisenberg, A. (1996) Privacy and Data Collection on the Net. *Scientific American*, 274 (March), 120.

Fabos, B. (1999) The Price of Information: Critical Literacy, Education, and Today's Internet. in S. Jones (ed.) *Doing Internet Research: Critical Issues and Methods for Examining the Net* (pp. 839–870). Thousand Oaks, CA: Sage Publications.

Fahey, T. (1994) *Net.speak: The Internet Dictionary*. Indianapolis, IN: Hayden Press.

Feig, B. (1989) How to Run a Focus Group. *American Demographics*. (December) 36–37.

Flower, J. (1994) Network Confidentiality. *New Scientist*, 144 (October 8), pp. 26–30.

Forester, T. (1992) Megatrends or Megamistakes?: What Ever Happened to the Information Society?. *The Information Society*. V. 8. N. 3. July-September. 133–146.

Gaiser, T.J. (1997) Conducting On-Line Focus Groups: A Methodological Discussion. *Social Science Computer Review*. 15 (2), pp. 135–144.

Gaiser, T.J. (2000) "An Analysis of the Emerging Social Forms in Cyberspace." Unpublished dissertation available through UMI Dissertation Services (UMI Number 9981617).

Gaiser, T. J. (2008) "Online Focus Groups". in Nigel Fielding, Ray Lee and Grant Blank (eds.) *Handbook of Online Research Methods*, London: Sage Publications.

Garton, L., Haythornthwaite, C. and Wellman B. (1999) Cybertalk and the method of instances. in S. Jones (ed.) *Doing Internet Research: Critical Issues and Methods for Examining the Net*. Thousand Oaks, CA: Sage Publications.

Gibson, D., Aldrich, C. and Prensky, M. (2007) *Games & Simulations in Online Learning: Research & Development Frameworks*. Hershey. PA: Information Sciences Publications.

Giles, J. (2005) Internet encyclopedias go head to head. *Nature*. 438, pp. 900–901.

Goffman, E. (1959) *The Presentation of Self in Everyday Life*. New York, NY: Anchor Books.

Grossman, D. (1996) *On Killing: The Psychological Cost of Learning to Kill in War & Society*. Boston, MA: Little, Brown & Co.

Grossman, D. and Degaetano, G. (1999) *Stop Teaching Our Kids to Kill: A Call to Action Against TV, Movie and Video Game Violence*. New York, NY: Crown.

Hahn, C. (2008) *Doing Qualitative Research Using Your Computer: A Practical Guide*. Los Angeles, CA: Sage Publications.

Harvey, G. (2004) *Windows XP for Dummies*. Hoboken, NJ: Wiley.

Healey, J.F. (1996) *Statistics: A Tool for Social Research*. 4th ed. Belmont, CA: Wadsworth Publishing.

Henderson, L. (2007) Shaping the Research Agenda with Cyber Research Assistants. in D. Gibson, C. Aldrich and M. Prensky (eds.) *Games & Simulations in Online Learning: Research & Development Frameworks* (pp. 366–385). Hershey, PA: Information Sciences Publishing.

Herring, S. (1996) Linguistic and Critical Analysis of Computer-mediated Communication: Some Ethical and Scholarly Considerations. *The Information Society*, 12, pp. 153–168.

Hewson, C., Yule, P., Laurent, D. and Vogel, C. (2003) *Internet Research Methods: A Practical Guide for the Social and Behavioral Sciences*. London: Sage Publications.

Hine, C. (2000) *Virtual Ethnography*. London: Sage Publications.

Howard, P.N. and Jones, S. (eds.) (2004) *Society Online: The Internet in Context*. Thousand Oaks, CA: Sage Publications.

Imparl, S. (2006), *Internet Law: The Complete Guide*. North Vancouver, BC: STP Special Technical Publishers.

Ito, M. (1996) Theory, Method, and Design in Anthropologies of the Internet. *Social Science Computer Review*, 14 (1), pp. 24–26.

Jacobs, G.E. (1999) People, Purpose, Practices: Insights from Cross-Disciplinary Research into Instant Messaging, in S. Jones (ed.) *Doing Internet Research: Critical Issues and Methods for Examining the Net* (pp. 467–490). Thousand Oaks, CA: Sage Publications.

Jelen, B. (2007) *Charts and Graphs for Microsoft Office Excel 2007*. Indianapolis, IN: Que Publishing.

Jones, S. (ed.) (1995) *CyberSociety: Computer-Mediated Communication and Community*. Thousand Oaks, CA: Sage Publications.

Jones, S. (ed.) (1999) *Doing Internet Research: Critical Issues and Methods for Examining the Net*. Thousand Oaks, CA: Sage Publications.

Kendall, L. (1999) The Conduct of Qualitative Interviews: Research Questions, Methodological Issues, and Researching Online, in S. Jones (ed.) *Doing Internet Research: Critical Issues and Methods for Examining the Net* (pp. 133-150). Thousand Oaks, CA: Sage Publications.

King S. (1996) Researching Internet Communities: Proposed Ethical Guidelines for the Reporting of Results. *The Information Society*, 12, pp. 119–128.

Kirk, J. (2006) AOL search data reportedly released. *MacWorld*. May 2008. http://www.macworld.com/article/52252/2006/08/www.idgconnect.com

Knowles, A.K. (ed.) (2008) *Placing History: How Maps, Spatial Data and GIS are Changing Historical Scholarship*. New York, NY: ESRI Press.

Kozol, J. (1988) *Rachel and Her Children: Homeless Families in America*. New York, NY: Ballantine Books.

Kraft, J.F. (1987) *Women, Computers, and Information Work*. Dissertation, The American University. UMI Dissertation Number AAT 8802771.

Krisnamurthy, S. (2004) The Ethics of Conducting E-Mail Surveys, in E. Buchanan, *Readings in Virtual Research Ethics: Issues and Controversies* (pp. 114–129). Hershey, PA: Information Science Publishing.

Lai, P.C. and Mak, A.S.H. (eds) (2007) *GIS for Health and the Environment*. Berlin: Springer.

Lawless, K.A. and Schrader, P.G. (1999) Where Do We Go Now?: Understanding Research on Navigation in Complex Digital Environments, in S. Jones (ed.) *Doing Internet Research: Critical Issues and Methods for Examining the Net* (pp. 267–296). Thousand Oaks, CA: Sage Publications.

Lawson, D. (2004) Blurring the Boundaries: Ethical Considerations for Online Research Using Synchronous CMC Forums, in E. Buchanan (ed.) *Readings in Virtual Research Ethics: Issues and Controversies* (pp. 80–100). Hershey, PA: Information Science Publishing.

Lewins, A. and Silver, C. (2007), *Using Software in Qualitative Research: A Step-by-Step Guide*. London: Sage Publications.

Maczewski, M., Storey, M.A. and Hoskins, M. (2004) Conducting Congruent, Ethical, Qualitative Research in Internet-Mediated Research Environments, in E.A. Buchanan, (ed.) *Readings in Virtual Research Ethics: Issues and Controversies*. Hershey, PA: Information Science Publishing.

Mann, C. and Stewart F. (2000) *Internet Communication and Qualitative Research: A Handbook for Researching Online*. London: Sage Publications.

Markham, A.N. (1998) *Life Online: Researching Real Experience in Virtual Space*. New York, NY: AltaMira Press.

Martineau, H. (1989) *How to Observe Morals and Manners*. New Brunswick, NJ: Transaction.

Miles, M.B. and Huberman, A.M. (1994) *Qualitative Data Analysis: Expanded Sourcebook*. Thousand Oaks, CA: Sage Publications.

Mortensen, E.M. (1999) Of a Divided Mind: Weblog Literacy, in S. Jones (ed.) *Doing Internet Research: Critical Issues and Methods for Examining the Net* (pp. 449–466). Thousand Oaks, CA: Sage Publications.

Nardi, B.A. (1996) Cyberspace, Anthropological Theory, and the Training of Anthropologists. *Social Science Computer Review*, 14 (1), pp. 34–35.

Nassr-Charlebois, C. (1990) *Gender Influences in the Classroom: Interaction of Young Children Using Computers*. Dissertation, University of Windsor, Canada. UMI Dissertation Number AAT MM61876.

Nelkin, D. (1994) Forbidden Research: Limits to Inquiry in the Social Sciences, in E. Erwin, S. Gendin and L. Kleiman (eds) *Ethical Issues in Scientific Research: An Anthology* (pp. 355–370). New York, NY: Garland Press.

Neustadtl, A., Robinson J.P. and Kestnbaum, M. (2002) Doing Social Science Research Online, in B. Wellman and C. Haythornthwaite (eds) *The Internet in Everyday Life* (pp. 186–211). Malden, MA: Blackwell Publishing.

Norton, P. and Sprague, D. (2001) *Technology for Teaching*. Needham Heights, MA: Allyn & Bacon.

Ormsby, T. (2001) *Getting to know ArcGIS Desktop*. New York, NY: ESRI Press.

Penrod, D. (2007) *Using Blogs to Enhance Literacy: The Next Powerful Step in 21st-century Learning*. Lanham, MD: Rowman & Littlefield.

Prensky, M. (2006) *Don't Bother Me Mom – I'm Learning*! St. Paul, MN: Paragon House.

Reynolds, P.D. (1982) *Ethics and Social Science Research*. Englewood Cliffs, NJ: Prentice-Hall.

Rheingold, H. (1993) *The Virtual Community: Homesteading on the Electronic Frontier*. Reading, MA: Addison-Wesley Publishing.

Richards, L. and Richards, T. (1991) Computing in Qualitative Analysis: A Healthy Development? *Qualitative Health Research*, 1 (May), pp. 234–262.

Rifkin, J. (1995) *The End of Work: The Decline of the Global Labor Force and the Dawn of the Post-Market Era*. New York, NY: G.P. Putnam's & Sons.

Roberts, L., Smith, L. and Pollock, C. (2004) Conducting Ethical Research Online: Respect for Individuals, Identities and the Ownership of Words, in E. Buchanan (ed.) *Readings in Virtual Research Ethics: Issues and Controversies*. (pp. 156–173). Hershey, PA: Information Science Publishing.

Sapsford, R. and Jupp, V. (eds) (1996) *Data Collection and Analysis*. Thousand Oaks, CA: Sage Publications.

Sauers, M.P. (2006) *Blogging and RSS: A Librarian's Guide*. Medford, NJ: Information Today.

Schuyler, E., Gibson, R. and Walsh, J. (2005) *Mapping Hacks*. Sebastopol, CA: O'Reilly.

Seale, C.F. (ed.) (2004) *Researching Society and Culture* (2nd edition). London: Sage Publications.

Seo, M. and Barrett, L.F. (2007) Being Emotional During Decision Making, Good or Bad?: An Empirical Investigation. *Academy of Management Journal*, 50 (4), pp. 923–940.

Sharf, B.F. (1999) Beyond Netiquette: The Ethics of Doing Naturalistic Discourse Research on the Internet, in S. Jones (ed.) *Doing Internet Research: Critical Issues and Methods for Examining the Net*. Thousand Oaks, CA: Sage Publications.

Shrader-Frechette, K.S. (1994) *Ethics of Scientific Research*. Lanham, MD: Rowman & Littlefield.

Sieber, J.E. (1992) *Planning Ethically Responsible Research: A Guide for Students and Internal Review Boards*. Newbury Park, CA: Sage Publications, (see also Participant Commentary – Do the Ends Justify the Means?: The Ethics of Deception in Social Science Research. Online Ethics Center at the National Academy of Engineering. http://www.onlineethics.diamax.com/CMS/research/rescases/gradres/gradresv1/justify/justify-c1.aspx accessed October 2007.)

Sinton, D.S. and Lund, J.J. (eds) (2007) *Understanding Place: GIS and Mapping across the Curriculum*. New York, NY: ESRI Press.

Smedinghoff, T.J. (1996a) Copyrights in Digital Information, in T.J. Smedinghoff (ed.) *Online Law: The SPA's Legal Guide to Doing Business on the Internet* (pp. 137–152). Reading, MA: Addison-Wesley Developers Press.

Smedinghoff, T.J. (1996b) Online Rights of Copyright Owners, in T.J. Smedinghoff (ed.) *Online Law: The SPA's Legal Guide to Doing Business on the Internet* (pp. 155–165). Reading, MA: Addison-Wesley Developers Press.

Smedinghoff, T.J. (1996c) Online Rights of Copyright Users, in T.J. Smedinghoff (ed.) *Online Law: The SPA's Legal Guide to Doing Business on the Internet* (pp. 169–190). Reading, MA: Addison-Wesley Developers Press.

Smith, M.A. (1992) *Voices from the Well: The Logic of the Virtual Commons*. Master's Thesis, University of California, Los Angeles.

Squire, P. (1988) Why the 1936 Literary Digest Poll Failed. *The Public Opinion Quarterly*, 52 (1) (Spring), pp. 125–133.

Staples, W. (2000) *Everyday Surveillance: Vigilance and Visibility in Postmodern Life.* Lanham, MD: Rowman & Littlefield.

Steinkuehler, C. (1999) Cognition and Literacy in Massively Multiplayer Online Games, in S. Jones (ed.) *Doing Internet Research: Critical Issues and Methods for Examining the Net* (pp. 611–634). Thousand Oaks, CA: Sage Publications.

Stern, S.R. (2003) Encountering Distressing Information in Online Research: A consideration of legal and ethical responsibility. *New Media & Society,* 5 (2), pp. 249–266.

Stern, S.R. (2004) Studying Adolescents Online: A Consideration of Ethical Issues, in E. Buchanan (ed.) *Readings in Virtual Research Ethics: Issues & Controversies.* Hershey, PA: Information Science Publishing.

Strauss, A. and Corbin, J. (1990) *Basics of Qualitative Research: Grounded Theory Procedures and Techniques.* Newbury Park, CA: Sage Publications.

Tapscott, D. and Williams, A.D. (2006) *Wikinomics: How Mass Collaboration Changes Everything.* New York, NY, Penguin.

Thomas, A. (1999) Community, Culture, and Citizenship in Cyberspace, in S. Jones (ed.) *Doing Internet Research: Critical Issues and Methods for Examining the Net* (pp. 671–698). Thousand Oaks, CA: Sage Publications.

Turkle, S. (1984) *The Second Self: Computers and the Human Spirit.* New York, NY: Simon & Schuster.

Turkle, S. (1995) *Life on the Screen: Identity in the Age of the Internet.* New York, NY: Simon & Schuster.

Walker, B.L. (1993) Computer Analysis of Qualitative Data: A Comparison of Three Packages. *Qualitative Health Research,* 3, pp. 91–111.

Walther, J.B., Anderson, J.F. and Park, D.W. (1994) Interpersonal Effects in Computer-Mediated Interaction: A Meta-Analysis of Social and Anti-Social Communication. *Communication Research,* 21 (4) pp. 460–479.

Weisband, S.P., Schneider, S.K. and Connolly. T. (1992) Participation Equality and Influence: Status Effects in a Computer-Mediated Decision Making Group. In *Fourth Annual Meeting of the American Psychological Association,* San Diego, CA.

Weitzman, E.A. and Miles, M.B. (1995) *Computer Programs for Qualitative Data Analysis.* Thousand Oaks, CA: Sage Publications.

White, P. "Email Interviews." (2005) http://www.webpronews.com/topnews/2005/07/27/email-interviews

Williams, F., Rice, R.E. and Rogers, E.M. (1988) *Research Methods and the New Media.* New York, NY: Free Press.

Witmer, D.F., Colman, R.W. and Katzman, S.L. (1999) Measuring INTERNET Audiences: Patrons of an On-line Art Museum. in S. Jones (ed.) *Doing Internet Research: Critical Issues and Methods for Examining the Net.* Thousand Oaks, CA: Sage Publications.

Wittel, A. (2000, January) Ethnography on the move: From field to net to Internet [23 paragraphs]. Forum Qualitative Sozialforschung/Forum: *Qualitative Social Research* [On-line Journal], 1 (1) Available at: http://www.qualitative-research.net/fqs-texte/1-00/1-00 wittel-e.htm (accessed on 7 March, 2007).

Zuboff, S. (1988) *In the Age of the Smart Machine: The Future of Work and Power.* New York, NY: Basic Books.

Zubrow, D.M. (1989) *Gender Differences and Learning to Compute: A Socialization Perspective.* Dissertation, Carnegie-Mellon University. UMI Publication number: AAT 9023439.

American Treasures of the Library of Congress. Dewey Defeats Truman, in the *Chicago Daily Tribune.* http://www.loc.gov/exhibits/treasures/trm145.html (accessed 21 March 2007).

INDEX

Supporting researchers for more than forty years

Research methods have always been at the core of SAGE's publishing. Sara Miller McCune founded SAGE in 1965 and soon after, she published SAGE's first methods book, Public Policy Evaluation. A few years later, she launched the Quantitative Applications in the Social Sciences series – affectionately known as the "little green books".

Always at the forefront of developing and supporting new approaches in methods, SAGE published early groundbreaking texts and journals in the fields of qualitative methods and evaluation.

Today, more than forty years and two million little green books later, SAGE continues to push the boundaries with a growing list of more than 1,200 research methods books, journals, and reference works across the social, behavioral, and health sciences.

From qualitative, quantitative, mixed methods to evaluation, SAGE is the essential resource for academics and practitioners looking for the latest methods by leading scholars.

www.sagepublications.com